CLUES FROM
THE PAST:

A Resource Book on Archeology

CLUES FROM THE PAST:

A Resource Book on Archeology

Edited by Pam Wheat and Brenda Whorton
Illustrated by Eileen Thompson

A Publication in Cooperation with the Texas Archeological Society
Hendrick-Long Publishing Co.
Dallas, Texas 75225-1123

ACKNOWLEDGEMENTS

We wish to express our appreciation to those who have contributed so generously to this special project of the Texas Archeological Society. The efforts of many people are reflected in the publication. It began as an Education Committee project encouraged by Dr. Grant Hall, who served as President of TAS when the work began. The project soon required the expertise and assistance of many people, all of whom are interested in providing an understanding of the value of archeology. Contributors include:

Jim Couzzourt   Carol Kehl
Nelda Cranford   Frances Meskill
Joan Few   Robert Turner

Maps were drawn by Paul Lorrain, and point types were drawn by Jay Whorton.

Careful review and commentary were graciously extended by Dr. Dee Ann Story, Dr. S. Alan Skinner, Dr. E. Mott Davis, Robert Mallouf, Pat Mercado-Allinger, Mark Parsons, J. B. Sollberger, and Dr. Jim Mitchell. Numerous teachers also critiqued early drafts in order to make the volume more useful in the classroom. Sincere appreciation goes to Helen Simons from the Office of the State Archeologist for her many hours of editing the multiple drafts of this work.

We would also like to thank our families who assisted and supported us in many ways: Joe, Jim, Kathy, Jim, Jeff, and Jay.

Cover photo by Prince McKenzie

Library of Congress Cataloging-in-Publication Data

Wheat, Patricia.
    Clues from the past : a resource book on archeology /
edited by Patricia M. (Pam) Wheat and Brenda Whorton :
illustrated by Eileen Thompson.
        p. cm.
    "A publication in cooperation with the Texas Archeol-
ogical Society."
    Includes bibliographical references and index.
    Summary: Surveys cultural time periods, antiquities, and
archeological sites in Texas and discusses the preservation
and study of such sites and the value of archeology in
general.
    ISBN 0-937460-65-6
    1. Archaeology--Methodology--Juvenile literature. 2.
Texas--Antiquities--Juvenile literature. 3. Indians of North
America--Texas--Antiquities--Juvenile literature. (1. Ar-
chaeology--Methodology. 2. Texas--Antiquities. 3. Indians of North America--Texas--Antiquities.) I. Whorton,
Brenda, 1942- , II. Title, III. Series: Thompson, Eileen,
1947-   Ill.
    CC75.W45 1990
    930.1--dc20   90-4991
                                               CIP
                                               AC

Design and Production
Sue Greaves   Tempe, Arizona

HENDRICK-LONG PUBLISHING COMPANY
Dallas, Texas 75225-1123

CLUES FROM THE PAST:

A Resource Book on Archeology

CONTENTS

INTRODUCTION

Archeology is a discipline which helps us learn about the human past. The methods of an archeologist are those of a scientist—hypothesis, data collection, analysis, and interpretation. Archeologists enrich our view of history and prehistory as they add information to the story of people who have lived in Texas for the past 12,000 years.

The goals of this publication are to spark an appreciation of past cultures and to encourage recording and preservation of archeological sites. Information about the early cultures will be presented along with activities which parallel the process used by archeologists.

Archeology expands cognitive skills by demanding problem solving and critical thinking. It also fosters a respect for nature, an unbiased study of foreign customs, and the on-going questioning of data. The integration of academic subjects occurs naturally in archeology with the combination of concepts from social studies, methodology from science, computation from mathematics, writing from language arts, and replication from fine arts.

The following sections are presented as a collection from which one can choose activities and information to suit special needs and interests. Section I relates the process used in archeological investigations. Section II chronicles the cultural history of the many diverse regions of Texas and provides the archeological perspective which augments historical accounts. Section III contains activities presented in a sequence to teach the archeological process. At the beginning of the third section a comprehensive ten-lesson unit is recommended for an intensive look at archeology. In addition separate activities offer a wide variety of choices. Throughout the text words with specialized meanings are set in bold type and defined in the Glossary.

Photo by Roseanna Henna

Section I

ARCHEOLOGICAL METHODS

Photo by Karen Collins

ARCHEOLOGICAL METHODS

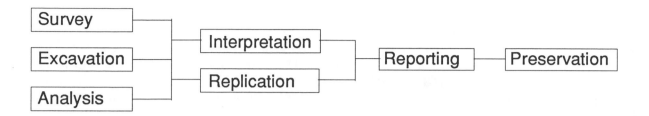

A. INTRODUCTION

As archeologists investigate a site, certain methods are used to ensure a consistent scientific approach. This process is illustrated in the flow chart above. An investigation of a site may end with a survey and report if there is sparse evidence or if the site is well-protected. However, when excavation takes place, analysis, interpretation, and reporting must occur.

The process of archeology has been broken apart artificially so that the methods may be discussed and, later, classroom activities presented which parallel each topic. The synopsis of methods is intended to serve as an introduction only, and additional references are listed with the activities. You may return to this methods section as you introduce activities which fall within each topic.

Photo by Brenda Whorton

SURVEY

You've decided you're interested—where do you go?

While the remains of early people are sometimes visible, as with Greek temples or Mayan pyramids, most clues from past cultures are buried. One way **sites** are found is by chance. A farmer or outdoorsman comes upon an object which is recognized as an **artifact**. He often reports the find to a museum, university, or local archeological society to get assistance in identifying the object. Recognition of artifacts in this way is a tremendous aid to archeologists. When archeologists begin systematically to **survey** a region, these chance finds serve as a starting point.

Archeologists also review the historical records of an area. These archival documents include maps, deed records, journals, photographs, and newspapers. Records supply many details about land use and often lead archeologists to sites which have been abandoned or overgrown.

Sometimes special techniques are used to locate sites. These techniques utilize the latest scientific inventions which might be applicable. Some of these techniques are use of aerial photography and **magnetometry**.

The pedestrian survey is probably the most common form of survey used. When walking an area in search of sites, the archeologists notice the **ecology** of the landscape. The environment and how early people might have responded to it are important clues for finding sites. Changes in vegetation often suggest areas to investigate. A review of the landscape allows archeologists to predict the location of sites which were near a water source, close to fertile soil, in a defensible area, or on a trail.

Photo by Jim Whorton

Sites can be categorized by use. The following types can be found: occupation sites, where people lived; special activity sites, such as tool making or food processing areas; kill sites, where many animals were killed and butchered; rock art sites containing painted or pecked designs; and cemeteries, where the dead were buried.

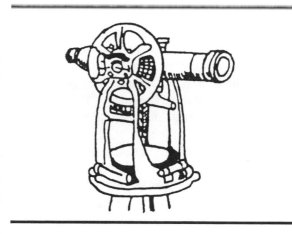

Every site should be reported to the institution responsible for compiling a secure data base, so that researchers will have current information about sites. Each site is assigned a reference number when it is recorded with the appropriate institution, which in Texas is the Texas Archeological Research Laboratory. The site numbering system was established by the Smithsonian Institution and is trinomial. A sample site designation might be 41 HR 1000. Within this number, 41 stands for the state of Texas, HR is Harris County, and 1000 is the one-thousandth site to be recorded at the agency. Site numbers are assigned as they are reported. (See Information for Site Reporting in the Appendix.)

To the Teacher

There are many procedures used by archeologists in the field which students can practice in the classroom. Observation, survey, and mapping techniques can be applied indoors and outdoors.

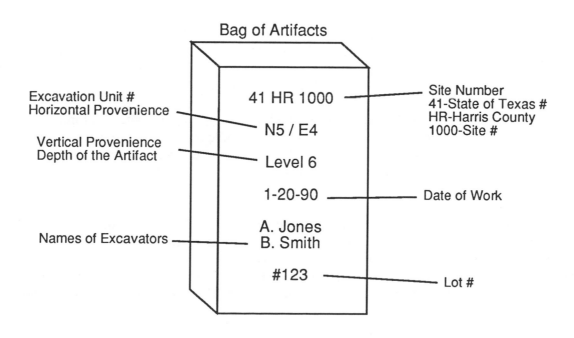

Bag of Artifacts

Excavation Unit #
Horizontal Provenience — 41 HR 1000 — Site Number
41-State of Texas #
HR-Harris County
1000-Site #

N5 / E4

Vertical Provenience
Depth of the Artifact — Level 6

1-20-90 — Date of Work

Names of Excavators — A. Jones
B. Smith

#123 — Lot #

EXCAVATION

Now that you've found a site, are you ready to get your hands dirty?

Since remains of past cultures are often buried, excavation is the primary technique used by archeologists in uncovering the past. The location of a site may have been discovered by chance or in a formal archeological survey. Before a recorded site is excavated a research design, which is a plan for studying the site, must be prepared. Laboratory analysis of the materials recovered from the site and a report of the findings of this analysis must follow excavation.

Currently conservation ethics are being applied to archeological sites. That is, unless a site (1) is threatened with destruction by natural or man-made causes or (2) will contribute significantly to a research question, the site should be left alone. Archeologists believe that technological advances in the future will enable scientists to learn much more from sites than can be learned today. Preservation of archeology today means that sites will be preserved for future generations.

The steps for systematic excavation include:
  1) mapping the surface (**topographic** map) and locating the site on a USGS map,
  2) laying out a **grid** system including a **datum point** for horizontal and vertical measurements,
  3) recording exploratory test pits,
  4) completing excavation plans by units and trenching, and
  5) backfilling after excavation, leaving a marker in the bottom of the unit.

Because archeological excavation destroys the site, certain precautions must be taken to ensure accurate records. The goal of accurate notes is to record features, artifacts, and structures which will allow the patterns of human behavior to emerge from the data.

Within the overall **grid** system, units are labelled to allow easy designation. Each **unit** is carefully mapped at designated **levels** and each artifact and feature are drawn on the map to indicate their exact location. The **elevation** of each unit, feature, and artifact is also recorded to provide a vertical picture of the layers of cultural deposition. A **profile** is made of the strata as they appear in a unit wall.

Records for each excavation unit usually include (1) an archeological site data form, (2) a level map, (3) a map of the vertical profile, (4) descriptive notes, (5) a collection bag, and 6) photographs. Recording and collection of materials during excavation should be uniform and non-subjective. All observations are recorded and all cultural materials retained for analysis.

To the Teacher

Numerous classroom activities are provided in Section III to give students the experience of excavation techniques. Simulation investigations are valid methods for training. If you desire to have students work in the field, contact an archeological society, a museum, or a university in your area to observe or join an on-going investigation. The archeologists will make sure that responsible instruction and supervision are provided. Excavation of actual sites should not be initiated merely for training or without the direction and assistance of experienced archeologists.

ANALYSIS

So what have you got? Or how to tell a bone from a twig.

After artifacts are recovered from the field, the laboratory process begins. Close examination of materials and records in the lab allows the archeologist to develop a picture of the people who occupied the site. Careful recording and handling of materials are essential as the artifacts are cleaned, sorted, classified, and identified. Each bag of material is labelled by **provenience**. There should be a corresponding **level form** for each collection of materials from the field. These items (bag and form) are given a lot number to be entered into a master catalog.

CLEANING

After the bags are logged in, the cleaning process begins. Some thought should go into the process, since the residue adhering to all artifacts should be carefully evaluated. Could the residue indicate a food source (grain or fat) or a method of construction (glue or attachment)? In some instances artifacts should not be thoroughly cleaned, only bagged to preserve all remains. When it is clear that an artifact should be cleaned, it can be washed gently in water then laid out to dry. Items such as basketry, leather, decaying wood, fragile bone, cloth, or paper should be brushed with a soft brush or blown clean with an ear syringe. Caution must always be maintained to keep lot numbers with the artifactual remains.

CATALOGING

This is the stage at which an **inventory** of the materials is made. The materials should be divided into categories such as **lithics**, **ceramics**, glass, metal, **fauna**, and **flora**. These distinctions are based on the substance of the material itself and not on use or function at this point.

Specific artifacts (points, ceramics, coins, etc.) have **diagnostic** characteristics and should be bagged and labelled individually. Other materials too small or insignificant to catalog individually should be reassembled and counted or weighed for the inventory.

A typical catalog number might be   41 HR 1000
                                          N5 / E4-6-123

In this catalog number   41 HR 1000 = site number
                            N5 / E4 = excavation unit
                            6 = level
                            123 = artifact number

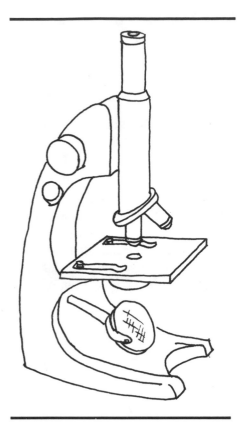

ANALYSIS

The next stage of laboratory work, artifact analysis, is fascinating and demanding. Each artifact tells its own story, which must be carefully identified and interpreted. Experience and study are important in evaluating the material remains which have been excavated. As many questions as possible are answered about the artifacts:

what they are,
how they were made and used,
who made or used them,
when they were used,
what is the source of the material from which they were made,
how they compare with similar items from other sites, and so on.

Each category of material has its own special traits and characteristics to be considered.

I. Lithics (stone)

In prehistoric sites the most easily recognized artifact is a stone tool. Stone artifacts can be divided into two main catagories, chipped and ground. Ground-stone tools include *manos, metates*, **celts**, **boatstones**, and weights. Chipped-stone tools include projectile points as well as **scrapers**, drills, and knives. Manufacture of stone tools is the oldest industry known to man, and evidence of the use of stone tools is found throughout the world. Types and styles of tools have been defined and redefined in a continuing dialogue between archeologists. Archeologists have compiled charts and manuals that allow comparison of types known to be associated with particular time periods.

II. Ceramics (fired clay)

Ceramics (objects made of fired clay) have been used for thousands of years and are frequently encountered in both prehistoric and historic sites. Pottery is analyzed on the basis of material, manufacturing technology, form, decoration, and function. Shape and size of an object or vessel can be determined if enough **sherds** are available for study.

In Texas most prehistoric pottery was made by the coil and scrape method. Most native pottery is unglazed, soft, and relatively fragile. Early Spanish and Mexican ware known as *majolica* is not so fragile and is glaze decorated. In the nineteenth century many European ceramic types appeared in Texas, including utility earthen ware, stoneware, and porcelain.

III. Glass

Glass artifacts are found mainly in historic sites. Even projectile points made from manufactured glass are found occasionally in historic **contexts**. Early glass artifacts include trade beads brought by the Spanish and French. European settlers added window glass, bottles, and jewelry to the items found in historic sites. Dates and functions of these objects can be found in specialized literature.

IV. Metal

Metals are generally indicative of historic time periods in Texas. Historic sites contain many metal artifacts including weapons, tools, construction items, and jewelry. Special care is needed in handling these materials, and advice of an expert should be obtained.

V. Fauna (bone)

Animal bone is found in both historic and prehistoric sites. The first step in analyzing bone is identification of species and marks that show human modification of the bone. Prehistoric sites most often contain the bones of wild animals with crude butchering marks. In historic sites the bone often comes from domesticated animals and, at later sites, the bone has usually been sawed rather than hacked. Bone is generally not well-preserved and careful handling is essential. Methods of bone preservation are frequently updated, so it is best to consult an expert.

VI. Flora (plants)

Important information about people and their lifeways comes from analysis of plants, including fibers, seeds, and pollen. The soil samples from excavation units can be submitted to a process known as **flotation**, or water separation. When submerged, the lighter plant (and some animal) materials float to the surface. They are then compared to known samples for identification or sent to botanists specializing in archeological analysis. Data regarding plants at a site are useful in reconstructing the environment and diet. Caution should be taken in projecting actual use of known resources from plant remains. Just because a specific plant pollen is present at a site does not mean that plant was used by the inhabitants.

To the Teacher

Opportunities to practice skills of analysis are defined in the Section III. They include replicating pottery and tools as well as classifying remains.

INTERPRETATION

Now that the clues are assembled, what do they mean?

Archeologists use the data collected from a site to develop a picture of how the people lived. One of the most basic questions to be resolved is the age of a site. Researchers need to know the age of finds so they can put the people into context. Dating helps archeologists correlate possible links between different peoples and predict how technology, ideas, and beliefs might have developed. Concepts of time and space are critical for the interpretation of archeological data.

DATING

A. Absolute Chronology: Age Expressed in Terms of Calendar Years

Absolute dating of materials is not a simple or precisely accurate task. Several samples should be dated to establish a range of dates. The chronometric methods which are considered reliable are listed below along with dateable materials and the chronological range at which each is useful.

potassium argon (K-Ar) / igneous materials / 5,000,000 to 400,000 years B.P. (before the present)

radiocarbon (Carbon 14) / organic materials / 60,000 B.P. to A.D. 1500

fission tracking / volcanic rock, glass / 1,000,000 to 100,000 B.P.

thermoluminescence / pottery, fired clay / 10,000 B.P. to present

dendrochronology / trees / 2,000 B.P. to present

archeomagnetic / baked clay / 2,000 B.P. to present

B. Relative Chronology: Sequential Ordering

Archeologists are able to estimate the dates of some remains by methods which lack precision. Methods used for relative dating include: (1) stratigraphy, (2) typology, and (3) cross dating.

1. The basic principle of **stratigraphy** is that the layers of the earth are superimposed one upon the other and remain in that order. Any object found in a lower stratum was deposited before objects in an upper stratum and, therefore, is older, provided the strata have not been disturbed. Certain occurrences, such as rodent activity and soil perculation can re-deposit artifacts, so care must always be taken in using this method of dating.

2. **Typology** is useful for analysis of artifacts. Most objects can be arranged by stylistic and manufacturing differences. This allows relative dating of the various artifacts and also dating of the stratum in which the respective artifacts were found.

3. **Cross dating** uses the date of one artifact to date the same kind of artifact in a different location. This technique assumes that artifacts with shared traits are likely of similar age.

To the Teacher

Activities in Section III are designed for students to use information collected by archeologists to develop an understanding of how people lived.

REPLICATING EARLY LIFEWAYS

What would it be like to live in the past?

Archeologists duplicate ancient technology and study art forms and manufacturing techniques in order to understand better the artifacts and patterns found in excavation. Replication means making or using an artifact as nearly as possible in the same way that early people made or used it. While one cannot test an ancient bow without potential damage to it, one can make and systematically experiment with a bow constructed from similar materials. These studies expand the interpretation of artifactual materials.

Some of the most famous modern replications are the voyages of Thor Heyerdahl on *Kon Tiki* and *Ra II*. These experiments tested the technological construction of the sea-going vessels and the theories of cultural contact and sea travel. Less complex experiments in replication include making shelters from natural materials and eating food from the wild. Any experiment which helps one "walk in the shoes" of another person provides valuable insight into people and their lifeways.

To the Teacher

Students learn about the daily life of early people by duplicating artifacts and testing their use. The process of construction is more important than the end result. The value of replication will be readily seen as the students come to appreciate human use of resources and human ingenuity throughout the ages.

REPORTING

What's the point of digging, if you don't tell someone about it?

The most important result of archeological investigations is sharing information about the past. Each piece of information gained from a site report adds to the still-incomplete record of how people once lived in Texas. Pulling together reports from several sites leads to a synthesis of information on a region.

Many mysteries still wait to be solved by persistant researchers who use archeological data to enrich the story of prehistory, a time when people left no written records of their own. Research questions are posed to ferret out more information about many topics, both prehistoric and historic. One continuing quest is for evidence of the earliest inhabitants of Texas, the **Paleoindians**. Artifacts made by Paleoindians have been found washed up on the beaches along the Gulf Coast, but very few of their campsites have been found in that region. Did these people, thousands of years ago, live on what is now the continental shelf, and have their campsites thus been inundated? What about those who followed the Paleoindians in time, the people of the Archaic period? They often used natural features such as rock shelters as habitation sites, but what kinds of dwellings did they build where no natural shelter was available? As the story of the past moves closer to us in time, into the Late Prehistoric period, even more detailed puzzles emerge. For example, what were the trading relationships between the nomadic tribes and the settled villager-farmers? Did the people of Northeast Texas trade with groups from as far away as the Big Bend region of Texas, or even from as far away as northern Mexico?

The historic period, which is covered by written records, also offers archeological mysteries to be solved. What is the exact location of Champ d'Asile, which was planned by Napoleon's aides as a base for the emperor's return to power? Records indicate a location on the Trinity River, but no remains have yet been found. Are the Twin Sisters cannon used at the Battle of San Jacinto still to be found? Have they long been overlooked in some slough or ravine because they are covered over with brush, or because they look like just so much rusted scrap metal? These and many other equally fascinating questions can be answered only by archeological investigation.

When a site is found and not recorded, the information that the site contains is lost. If a site is excavated, but the recovered remains are not analyzed and no report is ever published, the loss of information may be even greater. Excavation recovers important information, but it also destroys the **context** in which cultural remains are found. Therefore, every site that is discovered should be carefully recorded, and every site that is excavated must be reported.

To the Teacher

The importance of publishing, so that information can be shared with others, is a concept that students must understand. To emphasize this point, some type of reporting—oral, visual, or kinesthetic—should be part of every study of archeology. A unique form of reporting to consider is preparation of a display to promote public understanding of archeology. A project of this nature could be done for the classroom, neighborhood library, bank lobby, or museum. Preparation of an interpretive display forces the student to synthesize data and present a comprehensive view of the information. This technique represents a challenging mode of reporting.

PRESERVATION

Saving the past for the future.

It has become apparent in recent years that the destruction of archeological sites is robbing us of valuable information about our past. This destruction occurs because people do not understand the importance of archeological sites and isolated finds.

Relic collectors remove potential information when they pick up artifacts. If an artifact is removed from the **context** in which it was found, information related to the artifact is lost. Likewise, if a site is dug in an unscientific manner, destruction is complete. Collecting arrowheads or bulldozing mounds did not seem significant in the past. We know differently today.

The losses which have occurred in the past are multiplied due to population expansion and technological advances. Land modification occurs as communities expand, as roadways or waterways are needed, and as more fertile soil is cultivated. Although legal restraints can be used to protect some sites, cultural remains must be viewed as a scarce and nonrenewable resource to be preserved rather than squandered. Emphasis should be placed on locating sites, recording existing collections, and developing significant research designs to preserve the past for the future. (See Summary of the Antiquities Code of Texas in the Appendix.)

To the Teacher

Students can become involved in preservation issues through a simulation game, a debate, or an awareness campaign.

Section II

CULTURAL TIME PERIODS
IN TEXAS

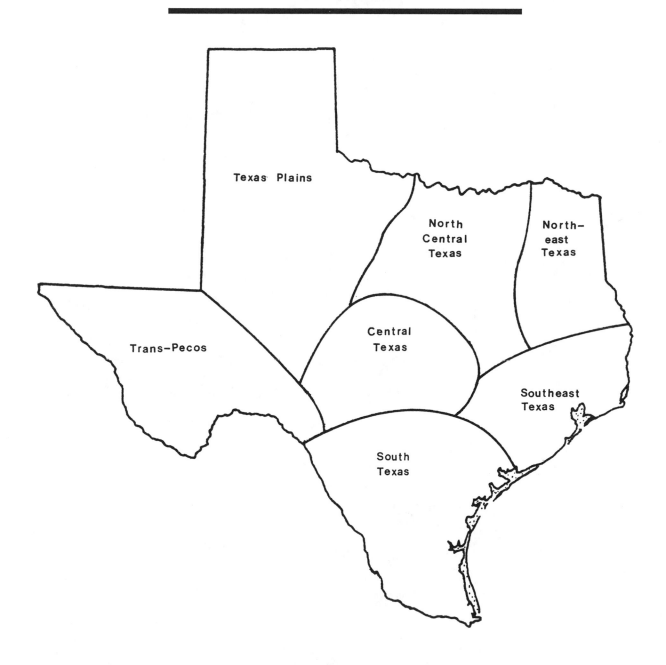

Cultural regions of Texas

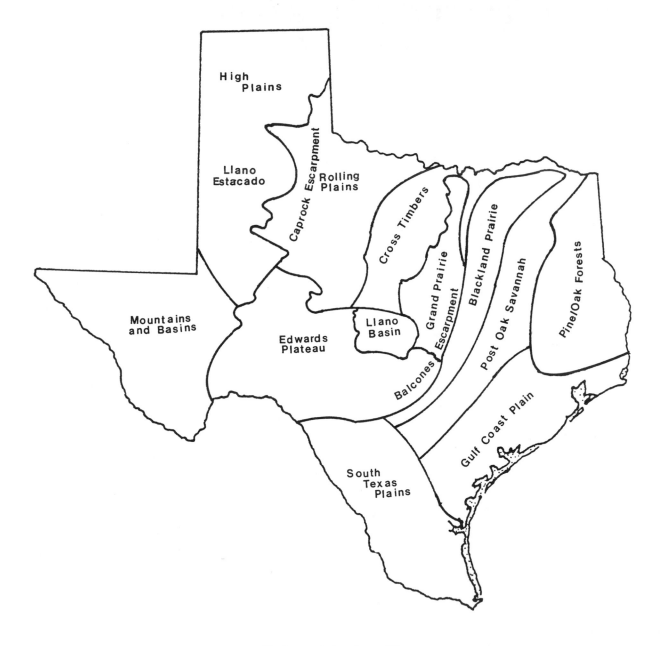

Environmental regions of Texas

ENVIRONMENTAL SETTING

The environmental setting of the state of Texas is truly one of contrasts and diversity. The landforms enclosed by the state's political boundaries include portions of at least three major physical divisions, the Rocky Mountain system, the Great Plains, and the Atlantic-Gulf Coastal Plain. In an important study, Frank Blair listed six different **biotic** provinces for the state. Plant and animal life is diverse, and the environments are influenced to a great extent by climate and topographic factors. The early inhabitants and later settlers experienced many variations on the Texas theme and adapted their lifestyles accordingly.

Prehistorians have identified at least seven general cultural regions within the state's 267,339 square miles. Each region developed cultural differences depending on the environment, topography, and movements of people and their ideas. It is essential to remember that prehistoric environments were vastly different at different points of time from the environmental picture of today. In addition, tremendous changes have occurred during the past 100 years due to modern land use and development.

THE TEXAS PLAINS

The Texas Plains region is divided into two distinct and physically separate zones, usually called the High Plains and the Rolling Plains. The latter consists of roughly 22,000 square miles of rolling prairies and rocky, broken "badlands" in northwestern Texas. The zone is bordered on the north by the Red River, on the west by the rugged Caprock Escarpment of the High Plains, and on the east by the Cross Timbers region. The zone's southern boundary is arbitrarily the north rim of the Colorado River Valley, where the Rolling Plains meets and blends almost imperceptibly with the southeastern Llano Estacado and western Central Texas region.

Most of the Rolling Plains is gently undulating prairie laced with small wooded streams emanating from the Caprock. Major streams in the region are the Red, the Brazos and its various forks, the White, and the Colorado rivers. Most of the soil in the prairie region is sandy. Limestone deposits are found in the southern part, along with prehistorically valuable deposits of flint-rich gravels. In some areas, vast sand sheets are held in barely stable condition by shin-oak belts and other trees. Mesquite **savannas** in uncultivated areas are common. Pecan and plum trees and other useful plants line some stream banks.

The almost 50,000 square miles of the High Plains consists of two arbitrary but, stubbornly separated territories, the Panhandle and the Llano Estacado. In local parlance, the Panhandle is the High Plains, while the Llano is the South Plains. The Panhandle as a political and geographic designation comprises the northern tier of 26 counties,

biotic - referring to animal and plant life.

savanna - a flat grassland.

playas - shallow, ephemeral, clay-bottomed basins which hold precipitation.

lithic - stone, or made from stone.

knapper - one who makes chipped stone tools.

scraper - a chipped stone tool used in processing vegetal or animal materials.

including the Canadian River Valley. Also included in the Panhandle boundary is the Palo Duro Canyon complex, though its southern or southeastern reaches intrude into the Llano Estacado and the Rolling Plains.

The Llano Estacado (Spanish for staked plains) ranges from about 30 miles north of Plainview southward to the northern rim of the Pecos River Valley, below Midland. Its western boundary extends into eastern New Mexico, where it forms the high, vertical eastern edge of the Mescalero Pediment, which dips down into the Pecos Valley. The southeastern limit of the Llano is difficult to delineate and equally difficult to see. It merges with the Rolling Plains and the western Central Texas and Trans-Pecos zones.

Water sources were critical to prehistoric inhabitants of the plains. Sites of all ages and cultures can be found near springs, streams, and **playas.** The Canadian River and the larger streams served as prehistoric "interstates," along which countless thousands of people crossed the region during the long years of prehistory.

Besides abundant water, prehistoric Indians found the plains rich in **lithic** resources, which was another necessity for survival. Alibates "flint" (agatized dolomite) has been an important stone-tool resource since the earliest reliably dated occupations of the Great Plains, and its wide distribution reflects its popularity among flint **knappers** for high-quality projectile points, knives, **scrapers,** and other tools. The Alibates Flint Quarries, situated in the Canadian River Valley in the north central Panhandle near Lake Meredith, is the only National Monument in Texas and represents one of the truly remarkable prehistoric resources of the Southwest. According to Mewhinney, "no other industrial site in the world has as long a record of continuous use lasting into modern times."

NORTH CENTRAL TEXAS

The North Central Texas region is bounded on the north by the Red River, on the west by the western edge of the Cross Timbers, on the east by the edge of the Blackland Prairie, and on the south by the Lampasas Cut Plain and the northern extension of the Balcones Escarpment. Nine major river drainages that provided advantageous camping sites for the aboriginal people were the Red River, the Wichita River, the Little Wichita River, three forks and main branch of the Trinity River, the Brazos River, and the upper reaches of the Sulphur River. During the past 20 years these drainages have seen major archeological projects which have provided insight into the long prehistoric and historic drama of human adaptation.

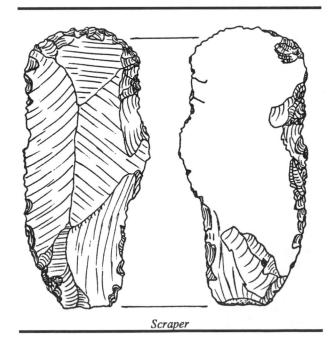

Scraper

North Central Texas is a transitional zone both archeologically and environmentally. Within the North Central Texas region two physiographic regions, the Great Plains province in the northwest and the Coastal Plain to the east and southeast, are represented. The weather in modern times is notorious for its sudden changes and enormous range in temperatures. This same pattern was undoubtedly true at different times in the long prehistoric period. Five vegetation zones that run generally north to south are the North Central Plains, the Western Cross Timbers, Grand Prairie, Eastern Cross Timbers, and the Blackland Prairie. Numerous studies have noted that the best **vegetal** and animal resources for prehistoric people were contained in the rich bottomlands of the river drainages.

vegetal - pertaining to plants.

CENTRAL TEXAS

Central Texas encompasses the eastern half of the Edwards Plateau, the Llano Uplift, most of the Lampasas Cut Plain, the southern end of the Grand Prairie, and the Blackland Prairie bordering the Balcones Escarpment. The geological formations rise from the relatively level prairies in the east to successively higher plateaus and rolling hills in the west. Altogether, the various aspects of the natural environment provided the resource base for the sequential human populations that adapted to the region.

Deeper soils with more moisture occur east of the uplift area in Central Texas, while thinner soils that cover the limestone uplift itself permit more rapid evaporation. Annual precipitation levels vary widely east to west across the region, and the number of frost-free days varies generally from north to south. The weather conditions are subject to sudden and drastic change.

Two broad biotic provinces divide the region into east and west subregions. The Texan province extends from the eastern forested region of Texas to the Balcones Escarpment, and the Balconian province continues westward to the Chihuahuan desert. Before grazing and land cultivation, the native vegetation of the Blackland Prairie was primarily tall grasses with post oak savanna

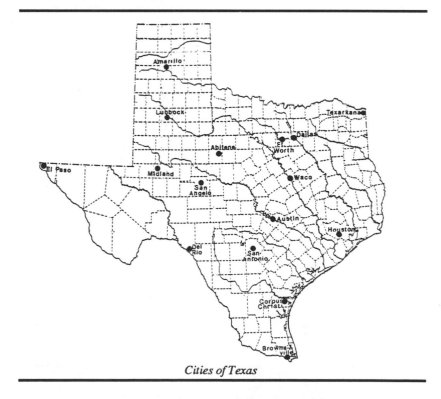

Cities of Texas

mott - a small stand of trees on a prairie.

flora - plants.

fauna - animals.

formations on sandy soils and some live oak **mottes.** Mixed and shortgrass prairies dotted by brush vegetation, oaks, cedar, and mesquite occur west of the Blacklands. Along the scarp zone evergreen and deciduous woodlands trail down the slopes and into ravines. Moist streamway environments of the region are dominated by oaks, elms, hackberries, pecan, and cottonwood.

In recent times 49 species of mammals have been identified in the Texan province and 57 in the Balconian. Evidence, however, suggests that prior to the end of the last Ice Age the **flora** and **fauna** were quite different for Central Texas during a period of cooler, more moist climatic conditions. Numerous faunal species became extinct at that time, while forests became smaller and previously dominant species disappeared.

NORTHEAST TEXAS

Environmentally, Northeast Texas is a part of the southeastern United States. All of the area lies within the Gulf Coastal Plain and is characterized by a cover of mixed pine and hardwood forests. The piney woods, which are native to most of Northeast Texas, are bordered on the west by the Post-Oak Savanna, which in turn is bordered by the Blackland Prairie in the northwestern part. Early Spanish missionaries to the area indicated the whole region was wooded except for small open spaces. Their comments 300 years ago also indicated the climate was not much different than it is today.

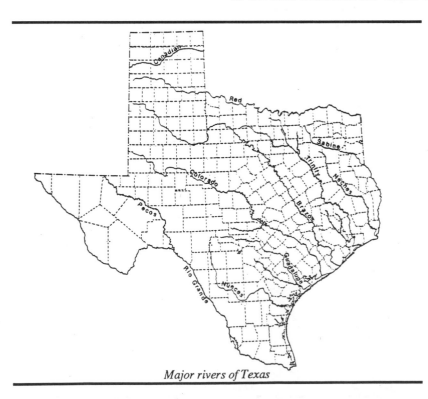
Major rivers of Texas

The region is bounded on the north by the Red River and is crossed by east-to-southeast flowing streams which, from north to south, are the Sulphur River, Cypress Creek or Bayou, the Sabine River, the Angelina River, and the Neches River. Northeast Texas is bordered on the southwest by the Trinity River. The map of Texas, which defines the regions described, shows Northeast Texas bounded on the south by the Kisatchie Escarpment. This escarpment crosses the upper parts of Newton, Jasper, Tyler, and Polk counties. Much of the area south of this line is normally considered

East Texas from a geographical standpoint. In late prehistoric times this boundary did in fact serve as an approximate dividing line between the Caddoan-speaking people to the north and the possibly **Atakapan**-speaking people to the south.

The elevation, which is near 600 feet in the northwest corner of the area, slopes gently downward toward the south and east. A belt of small hills extends from Cass County in the northeast to Anderson County in the west central part of Northeast Texas. These are the Weches Ironstone Hills and seldom are more than 300 feet in elevation above the surrounding terrain.

The weather in Northeast Texas is relatively mild, with winter temperatures in the north averaging 40° F and about 50° F in the south. Summer temperatures average about 80° F. Annual rainfall averages about 45 inches in the north to 48 inches in the southern region. The growing season between frosts is 235 to 240 days, which made the area hospitable for early development of **horticulture.**

SOUTHEAST TEXAS

The Southeast Texas cultural region extends along the upper Gulf Coast from the Sabine River to the lower Colorado River drainage. The width of the region runs approximately 100 miles from the coast inland. Late **Pleistocene** geologic history indicates that various rivers formed deltas which in turn joined to form a continuous plain. As the sea level rose with the melting of the ice sheets, this plain became divided into sections of estuaries, barrier islands, and the modern bays and deltas.

The region is not all flat prairies and marshes. Inland from the coast the soils are sandy and better drained. Here pine and hardwood forests top the slightly rolling terrain.

The major rivers of Southeast Texas, the Sabine, the Trinity, the San Jacinto, the Brazos, and the Colorado, provided routes for trade to Northeast and Central Texas. They also presented a potentially hazardous environment because of flooding in the lower reaches. In spite of the problems, however, these areas were exceptionally rich in floral and faunal resources necessary to support human habitation.

SOUTH TEXAS

The South Texas region is composed of five distinctive "bio-geographical" subareas: the Rio Grande Plain, the Rio Grande Delta, the Nueces-Guadalupe Plain, the Sand Sheet, and the Coastal Bend. Marked differences in human adaptation can be found within the subregions. From an archeological point of view, the Nueces-Guadalupe Plain and Coastal Bend areas are the best known and were the most favorable for prehistoric adaptation.

The Rio Grande Plain is located parallel to the river drainage between the Lower Pecos region and Cameron and Hidalgo counties. The climate is arid and subtropical, and few permanent water sources are located away from the river. Because of the plant and animal life available along river terraces, these were the areas most intensively occupied by prehistoric peoples. Plants such as prickly pear, **lechuguilla**, and **sotol** provided dietary staples in early times. The Rio Grande Plain is little-known archeologically, but it is apparent from **ethnohistoric** sources that it was frequented by many Indian groups.

The low-lying Rio Grande Delta subarea is situated in the southernmost section of Texas, mainly in Cameron and Hildalgo counties. Semiarid with extremely hot summers, this area proved to be a difficult environment in terms of resource acquisition for prehistoric peoples. The scant number of artifacts usually associated with very early human habitation suggests that some sections of the region were apparently unoccupied until about 3000 years ago.

Several river drainages dissect the largest subarea, the Nueces-Guadalupe Plain. With their wide range of resources, the river drainages were the places preferred by early Texans for visiting and camping. This situation is in marked contrast to the outlying savanna lands, where only a very marginal existence could be sustained. Much data from the area has emerged from investigations conducted in Live Oak and McMullen counties before the building of the Choke Canyon Dam.

No permanent surface water is present in the Sand Sheet area, a small section in the deep south of Texas. Semiarid and subtropical, most of the area is covered by a thin layer of sand that supports thorny brush. Abundant grasslands, however, are present in some sections, such as the King Ranch. In general, archeological information on the Sand Sheet subarea is quite limited.

The coastal area between the Colorado River and Baffin Bay makes up the fifth South Texas subarea, the Coastal Bend. Numerous archeological remains have been recovered in this ecologically diverse environment, which is the setting for estuary bays, coastal grasslands, and an extensive system of barrier islands. The frequency of cultural remains, along with recorded observations by early explorers and settlers, document repeated use of the Coastal Bend through time by both prehistoric and historic Indian groups. The climate here is subtropical, and subhumid in the northeast section.

TRANS-PECOS

The westernmost region of Texas is known as the Trans-Pecos. It is bordered on the west and south by the Rio Grande, on the north by

Digging sotol roots

the Texas and New Mexico state line, and across the east by an imaginary line running approximately 50 miles east of the Pecos River. The region encompasses environmental zones of mountains, foothills, basins, and rivers.

The archeologically rich Lower Pecos subregion is located in the lower Devil's River and Pecos River drainages. This area is especially well known because of research projects conducted before the filling of Amistad Reservoir. There, large rock shelters formed in the limestone cliffs protected early hunter-gathers and their unique art.

Principal mountain ranges include the Davis, Chisos, and Guadalupes, the latter capped by the highest point in Texas, Guadalupe Peak, at an elevation of 8,749 feet above sea level. It is interesting to note that the highland zones of these ranges were exploited by aboriginal people.

The Trans-Pecos region lies in the northern section of the Chihuahuan Desert, which is abundant in all the resources necessary for human survival. There is an impressive diversity in plants and animals. Flood plains are dominated by broadleaf trees and shrubs, while above 3,700 feet elevation broadleaf and coniferous forests predominate. The mid-elevation zone is a desert shrub environment with cacti, yucca, sotol, and lechuguilla providing many needed resources. So, rather than the harsh environment as it is often characterized, the Trans-Pecos has provided an abundant resource base capable of sustaining cultural development for thousands of years.

REFERENCES

Blair, W. Frank
  1950   The Biotic Provinces of Texas. *Texas Journal of Science* 2:93-117.

Bryant, Vaughn, and Harry J. Shafer
  1977   The Late Quaternary Paleoenvironment of Texas: A Model for the Archeologist. *Bulletin of the Texas Archeological Society* 48:1-25.

Gehlback, Frederick R.
  1985   *Structure and Succession of Woody Vegetation on the Northeastern Balcones Escarpment and Edwards Plateau of Texas*, edited by B.B. Amos and F.R. Gehlback. Baylor University Press, Waco, Texas, in press.

Gould, Frank W.
  1975   *Texas Plants: A Checklist and Ecological Summary*. Publications of Texas Agricultural Experiment Station, College Station, Texas.

Hill, Robert
  1901   *Geography and Geology of the Black and Grand Prairies, Texas*. Twenty-first Annual Report of the U.S. Geological Survey to the Secretary of the Interior, 1899-1900, Part 7.

Mewhinney, H.
  1965   Alibates Flint Quarry. *Texas Parks and Wildlife*. 23:20-25.

Map of the ice-free corridor from Beringia

Cultural Time Periods

PALEOINDIAN PERIOD
(before 6,000 B.C.)

For years spirited debate has raged around the origins of the first Americans. When they arrived, how they arrived, and from where they came are all highly debatable questions. During the last Ice Age, known as the Wisconsin glaciation, the land that now forms Siberia and Alaska was joined by a sizable land bridge called Beringia. Since huge quantities of the earth's water were frozen into the ice sheets, sea levels during that time were much lower and exposed land which today is submerged.

Early man and the Pleistocene animals that he hunted crossed between the two great continents. Geologists have developed time sequences demonstrating that during periods of cold Beringia would have been open to travel. In general it is felt that from 75,000 to 10,000 years before the present there were at least four periods during which passage would have been possible.

Once in Alaska, however, the early migrants found that the two massive ice sheets which covered much of North America presented a formidable obstacle. At certain periods an ice-free corridor opened between the two sheets extending from Alaska to Edmonton, Alberta, and the northern plains. The real problem, it seems, was getting through the unglaciated, inhospitable corridor to the plains.

Scientists have long pondered the possibility of **Paleoindian** migrations from Asia to the Americas by boat and by a southern route, entering the New World by way of South America. Although this route is plausible, the archeological record offers little evidence of coastal travel at that time. Perhaps future research on the continental shelf will offer more concrete evidence. Regardless of how they arrived, the Paleoindians spread throughout North, Central, and South America and in the process populated Texas for the first time.

The earliest Paleoindians conclusively recognized are identified by a distinctive fluted projectile point called the Clovis point. The name was derived from the locale near Clovis, New Mexico, where it was first found. A fluted projectile point has a relatively long channel flake removed from the lower central portion of the point, a technique which requires an especially high degree of skill. This point was **hafted** onto spears, lances, or darts and used to kill the Pleistocene **megafauna**, as well as smaller game. In a recent study of Clovis points in Texas, analysis revealed that the majority of Clovis finds are from the High Plains, although the type is represented throughout the state.

Paleoindian - late Pleistocene peoples in the Americas.

hafted - attached in a special way.

megafauna - large, now-extinct Pleistocene animals, such as the mammoth.

Mammoth

Clovis point   *Folsom point*   *Plainview point*

feature - cultural remains which stay together and are more complex than a single artifact.

B.P. - before the present, which is dated at 1950.

context - relationship of cultural remains to each other and to the surrounding soil deposits.

flaking - the way in which fracturing of stone produces needed tools and projectile points.

Two sites, Lewisville in Denton County and McFaddin Beach in Jefferson County, illustrate some of the problems of studying Clovis-period sites and artifacts. In the late 1960s a Clovis point was recovered in association with cooking-hearth **features** along the shore of Lake Lewisville. Material from the hearths produced radiocarbon dates of 37,000 **B.P.**, a date which caused a great deal of excitement and controversy in the archeological community. A retesting and reevaluation of the site data in 1981 found that the misleading early date was due to contamination of the dated sample by lignite. The investigators concluded that Lewisville represented a Clovis-period occupation; however, the search for pre-Clovis people remains an elusive but tantalizing goal. The McFaddin Beach site raises questions of interpreting data, because artifacts were discovered out of their original **context.** Artifacts recovered along the coastline have often been redeposited there after having been washed up from inundated lands, and information about the time period and the site from which they came remains unknown. The inundated lands were likely preferred coastal camping grounds during the Paleoindian period.

A second fluted point type, the Folsom, is thought to have been used by a later culture. A favored prey of these people was the large, extinct bison that became dominant after many of the megafauna diminished in numbers. The Folsom point is a somewhat smaller, thinner, and slightly different version of the Clovis point. The fluting scars, usually on both faces, are relatively longer on Folsom points, reaching almost to the tip, and some specimens have sharp-pointed basal ears. The **flaking** technique of Folsom points is often better and more delicate than that of Clovis points. The Adair-Steadman site, in Fisher County near Abilene, is a large Folsom campsite where early emphasis was on the manufacture of Folsom points. The site has produced invaluable information on the entire Folsom point-making process. At Bonfire Shelter in Val Verde County, Folsom hunters stampeded bison over a 70-foot-high cliff in perhaps three different jumps. Among other possible Folsom sites in the state are Kincaid Rockshelter near Sabinal and two sites near San Antonio.

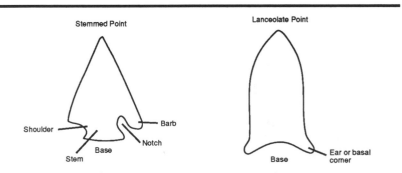

Terms used in describing projectile points (adapted from Turner and Hester 1985)

Cultural Time Periods

During the latter part of the Paleoindian period, a new culture called Plano developed. Several point styles, such as Plainview, Firstview, and Angostura, are grouped together as typical of this time period. The lanceolate-shaped projectile point continued to be used, but the technique of fluting was dropped. Populations of Plano hunters apparently increased, since Plano sites are more common than both Clovis and Folsom sites combined. A broader range of projectile point styles is evident, and the overall Plano stone and bone **tool kit** is more varied than those of the previous centuries. Material used for the tools is highly diversified and suggests that great distances were traveled by these people. The San Patrice point in East Texas, however, seems to have been manufactured from locally obtained flint.

Paleoindians have often been portrayed as avid hunters roaming over vast territories in pursuit of very large game animals. In fact, these Indians probably achieved a greater diversity in their diet than was once thought. Studies of vertebrate and other bone remains at Baker Cave in Val Verde County show that snakes, fish, and rodents, as well as larger mammals, were consumed. *Metates* used to grind seeds and other plants appear toward the end of this period in a few sites. The people used virtually every resource provided by their environment.

Burials representing the Paleoindian period from Bosque and Williamson counties have been studied. In the Horn Shelter site, a burial of a man and young child were accompanied by goods of a practical as well as ornamental nature. Along with knapping tools, an eyed needle, and a **shaft straightener,** all made of bone or antler, there were perforated canine-tooth pendants, modified turtle shells, and unperforated bird claws. Near Leander the burial of a woman, who was about 30 years-old at the time of death, was uncovered by archeologists. Once again the manner in which she was interred told of care and concern expressed by those who were close to her.

Some researchers postulate that toward the end of the Paleoindian period, Texas entered a prolonged dry spell, called the Altithermal. During the Altithermal, the average temperature rose and average rainfall diminished. Excavations and tests at deeply **stratified** sites showing long periods of occupation, such as the Lubbock Lake site, indicate that from roughly 6,500 to 7,500 years ago many of the state's regions underwent severe drought conditions. At Lubbock Lake soils deposited during this period have high concentrations of wind-blown sand and dust. The tall-grass prairie disappeared entirely during the Altithermal, and when the rains returned, short grasses prevailed, just as they do today. As the environment changed, so did the plants and animals inhabiting Texas—and so did the numbers and survival strategies of the Indians dependent on those resources.

tool kit - a collection of materials used in manufacturing points, scrapers, etc., as well as a few of those implements in both finished and unfinished state.

metate - stone slab upon which foods are ground or otherwise processed.

shaft straightener - a piece of stone or bone used to straighten dart or arrow shafts.

stratified - in layers.

San Patrice point

Shaft straightner

ARCHAIC PERIOD
(6,000 B.C. - 200 B.C. and later)

radiocarbon dating - a frequently used method based on measuring the decay of the radioactive isotope of carbon (C14) to stable nitrogen (N14).

atlatl - spear thrower.

midden - refuse or trash pile.

The cultural period that lasted the longest in Texas is the Archaic, which began around 6,000 B.C. It should be emphasized, however, that time and territorial boundaries of cultures are frequently arbitrary. Even if a cultural marker has been substantiated by an absolute dating technique, such as **radiocarbon dating**, cultures do not change overnight.

Generally speaking the Archaic was a period marked by changes in technology and survival strategies, along with changes in population densities and locations. Lanceolate-shaped points of the Paleoindian time period gave way to barbed or shouldered dart points, implying an almost universal preference for the **atlatl,** or throwing stick. Since the points **hafted** onto the spear were destined to be propelled and not jabbed, the barbs and shoulders provided a wider and deeper penetrating wound, and, by consequence a surer kill. It is thought that a hunter could hurl a spear about 70 yards (64 meters), but with an atlatl the spear could reach a distance of 150 yards (137 meters). Grinding tools became more common, indicating a greater dependence on vegetal foods, and the usually small Paleoindian firepits developed into large stone-lined hearths. In the western part of the state large burned-rock **middens** appeared, apparently the accumulated results of repeated mass cooking or baking of vegetal foods, such as yucca and sotol. Middens are essentially deposits of trash and are found in varying sizes and forms as an integral part of most sites. The large middens composed of fire-cracked or burned rocks, indicate intense use of earth ovens, stone-lined hearths, or boiling stones.

There is no evidence of horticulture in the Archaic, and permanent camps or settlements were apparently uncommon, though major base camps did occur. Any evidence for constructed shelters is rare. Archaic shelters were probably made of brush, grass, or hides and hastily thrown together. Burials indicate social and religious concerns and respect for the dead. Archeology has shown that burial customs ranged from limited cremation to fully extended interments in prepared, slab-lined crypts, with accompanying goods including weapons, tools, ornaments, and possible foodstuffs. In some areas rock **cairns** protected the remains from scavengers.

The Archaic is subdivided into three periods called the Early, Middle, and Late Archaic. Archeological investigations have so far revealed relatively few single-component

Atlatl showing method of use

cites (sites occupied by a people during only one period and not reoccupied by later peoples). Therefore, limited information on the Early and Middle Archaic periods is derived principally from studies of sites containing many levels of occupation.

Archeologists believe that, during the early years of the Archaic, populations were low and scattered, possibly because warming during the Altithermal made parts of the state, especially the western sections, undesirable for human habitation. The Indians were forced to accommodate their lifestyle to the drying conditions. One report suggests that bison were absent during the warm, dry period of the Early Archaic, so people of this time turned to other game for their dietary needs. Along most of the major river drainages the changed environment included more wooded bottomlands, which increased the hunting-gathering resource base. In many areas of the state rabbit, turtle, and deer evidently became the most desirable prey, since it is their remains which show up frequently in excavated sites. Also, fish bones and fresh-water shells indicate use of the waterways. Collection of nuts, seeds, and other edible plants rounded out the **subsistence** base.

Most of the sites known to date from this period are temporary campsites. They were reused on a seasonal basis or only from time to time. These sites typically yield projectile points and chipped-stone tools, such as knives and scrapers, that were used in food, hide, and wood processing. Ground-stone tools included *manos* and *metates*, used for grinding foods, hammer stones employed in tool making and other activities, and **Waco sinkers,** which may have been used for net weights or **bolas.**

During the Middle Archaic period, life appears to have become somewhat easier. Toward the end of the period, the environment once again changed in response to the end of the Altithermal. The weather became cooler, there was an increase in moisture, and the bison returned. Burned-rock middens emerge as a dominant archeological feature across a large central portion of the state. Large cemeteries with numerous burials also have been found, especially in Central Texas. In that region Pedernales points are typical artifacts. State-wide, stone and shell artifacts found at great distances from their origin hint of exchange networks and interaction between groups of different regions.

Judging from the archeological record, the Late Archaic

cairn - a mound of stones.

subsistence - means of support, especially food and clothing.

mano - a hand-held stone tool used to process foods.

bolas - stones attached to a rope used to catch animals by entangling the legs.

Waco sinker - a water worn pebble with notches on the ends, perhaps used as a sinker weight.

Use of mano and metate

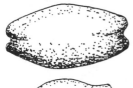

Waco sinker

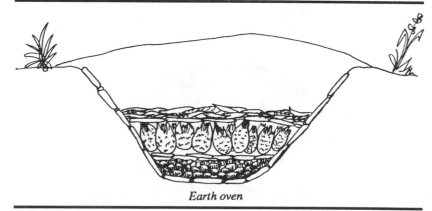

Earth oven

pictographs - painted art forms on rock.

Pedernales point

period witnessed a growth in population and intense cultural development within the major regions of Texas. Sites are more numerous and are found in many settings, from river bottom terraces to hill-top vantage points. Animal-bone remains vary from snake to bison, but the bison remains indicate that these beasts were not always available, even on the plains or in Central Texas. The nomadic Archaic Indian was a true hunter-gatherer, fully exploiting the resources of his area, and in his wanderings encountering the ideas and technology of other peoples.

In North Central Texas, archeologists have studied Late Archaic hamlets in which large depressions were a prominent feature. Located along the Elm Fork and Middle Trinity River drainages, these pits, generally oval in shape, averaged approximately 20 meters in length and 3 meters in depth. Analysis of remains has suggested that the pits were used for large-scale roasting activities and as cemeteries. Nuts were roasted after the fall harvest, while tubers were evidently roasted in the spring in order to preserve them for later use. This kind of large-scale activity has led researchers to conclude that spring and fall probably saw bands coming together for special ceremonies of harvest and exchange of resources.

The Trans-Pecos was another region which witnessed distinctive developments during the Late Archaic period. On the walls of some rock shelters in Val Verde County, Archaic artists painted vivid figures of humans, animals, and geometric shapes. The human figures are usually interpreted as shamans, or medicine men, whose sizes are as striking to modern visitors as they probably were to the ancient Texans. Renowned for its **pictographs,** Fate Bell Shelter in Seminole Canyon contained well-preserved artifacts such as netting, sandals, baskets, and snares, along with atlatl shafts, wooden digging sticks, and rabbit sticks. These kinds of perishable cultural remains add immeasurably to our understanding of human lifeways.

The close of the Archaic and the beginning of the Late Prehistoric period vary from region to region in the state. In general the cultural changes which signal the transition began in the Panhandle around A.D. 150 and slowly swept south, reaching the South Texas region by A.D. 800. In the eastern part of the state, especially the northeast, the use of pottery began as early as 200 B.C., a time which for that region

A pictograph from the Lower Pecos

delineates the end of the Archaic and the beginning of a period called the Early Ceramic. Because of the complexities and regional differences of the Late Prehistoric and Historic periods, seven regions of the state will be treated separately.

REFERENCES

Aten, Lawrence E.
>   1983   *Indians of the Upper Texas Coast.* Academic Press, New York.

Dillehay, Tom D.
>   1974   Late Quaternary Bison Population Changes on the Southern Plains. *Plains Anthropologist* 19(65):180-196.

Fiedel, Stuart J.
>   1987   *Prehistory of the Americas.* Cambridge University Press, Cambridge, England.

Martin, William A., and James E. Bruseth
>   1988   Wylie Focus Pits: A New Look at Some Old Features. *The Record* 42(3): 20-35. The Dallas Archeological Society, Dallas, Texas.

Meltzer, David J.
>   1987   The Clovis PaleoIndian Occupation of Texas: Results of the Texas Clovis Fluted Point Survey. *Bulletin of the Texas Archeological Society* 57:27-68.

Redder, Albert J.
>   1985   Horn Shelter Number 2: The South End, A Preliminary Report. *Central Texas Archeologist* 10:37-65. Baylor University Press, Waco, Texas.

Sandford, Dennis
>   1982   *Critical Review of Archaeological Evidence Relating to the Antiquity of Human Occupation in the New World.* Smithsonian Contributions to Anthropology, Vol. 30. Washington, D.C.

Turner, Ellen Sue, and Thomas R. Hester
>   1985   *A Field Guide to Stone Artifacts of Texas Indians.* Texas Monthly Press, Austin, Texas.

Word, James H. and Charles L. Douglas
>   1970   *Excavations at Baker Cave, Val Verde County, Texas.* Bulletin of the Texas Memorial Museum, 16:1-151.

Texas Plains

Cultural Time Periods

LATE PREHISTORIC PERIOD
(A.D. 150 - A.D. 1550)

The Late Prehistoric period on the Texas Plains began with the adoption of two technological innovations, the bow and arrow and pottery. These changes took place gradually and at different times in different areas. There is some evidence that the bow and arrow made its first Texas appearance on the High Plains. At Deadman's Shelter in Tule Canyon, small corner-notched arrow points, along with dart points and a very few ceramic **sherds,** have been dated to A.D. 147.

The bow seems to have entered the plains from the north, where radiocarbon dates and other evidence indicate its presence a century or two earlier. Pottery, on the other hand, may have first entered from the south, from Mexico via New Mexico and the El Paso area. The earliest plains pottery (from Deadman's Shelter) appears to be a plain, brown utilitarian ware related to types from the El Paso-New Mexico area. Another early pottery type, Woodland Cordmarked, is limited mainly to the Panhandle and may be almost as early as the brownwares.

Two major plains cultures, the Palo Duro and the Plains Woodland, are identified from the early part of the Late Prehistoric period. Each culture shows evidence of origins or major influences from other regions, and each seems to have remained on the High Plains for almost a thousand years.

Palo Duro Culture

Named for its widespread occurrences in the Palo Duro Canyon system and adjacent areas, the Palo Duro culture was composed of groups of hunter-gatherers who lived in much the same way as their Archaic predecessors. They made Late Archaic-style dart points, subsequently replaced by small corner-notched arrow points, and a distinctive basally notched, narrow-stemmed arrow point. Their sites are often littered with thin-slab *metates* and *manos* and burned rocks or boiling stones. The people utilized a plain brownware pottery similar to types from the **Mogollon** region, implying close ties with that cultural region.

Dates for Palo Duro occupations range from around A.D. 147 at Deadman's Shelter to as late as the mid-900s at Chalk Hollow in Palo Duro Canyon. The seeming disappearance of the Palo Duro culture has not been satisfactorily explained—perhaps because no disappearance took place. Like others in the Southwest, these people may have responded to environmental and cultural changes by adopting or

sherd - a fragment of pottery.

Mogollon - a prehistoric culture occupying a region of what is today is part of Arizona, New Mexico, Sonora, and Chihuahua.

Use of bow and arrow

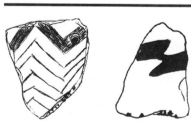

ceramic sherds

olla - a wide-mouthed ceramic jar.

tumpline - a strap slung across the forehead or chest to support a load carried on the back.

Tumpline in use

adapting new tools and survival strategies, such as becoming full-time bison hunters when the bison returned *en masse* to the plains around A.D. 1200.

Plains Woodland

The Plains Woodland people entered the Panhandle some time before A.D. 400, bringing with them tools and pottery reminiscent of better-studied, earlier Plains Woodland groups in Kansas, Nebraska, Oklahoma, and eastern Colorado. The Woodland manifestation in the Panhandle is a fairly late one, with arrow points dominating dart points and pottery already being used. The lifestyle is again essentially Archaic, with no dependable evidence of horticulture, permanent villages, or structures. Significant technological and cultural changes did not take place until very late in the period. Evidence of trade or other contacts is minimal, and Woodland peoples made heavy use of local resources. Their sites are littered with grinding tools and burned rocks, along with small rock-lined hearths, indicating extensive use of plant foods.

Woodland artifacts include a few medium-sized to small dart points and a variety of small, well-made, corner-notched arrow points, most of which were fashioned from Alibates agate. Ceramics are limited to a single vessel form, a large, wide-mouthed *olla* with a curved base and no discernible shoulder. The rounded base was useful for embedding the large jars in the Panhandle's sandy soils, and perhaps made the vessels easier to transport over long distances by a **tumpline** or net slung over the carrier's back.

The Woodland period on the Texas Plains has been little studied by archeologists, so dates are virtually nonexistent. A single Woodland pot sherd from the Tascosa Creek site, near Boys Ranch in Oldham County, has been dated to A.D. 520.

In the last 400 to 500 years of the Late Prehistoric period, changes took place rapidly and on a sweeping scale. As people of differing cultures made their way onto the plains in search of the returning bison, ideas, customs, and technologies were interchanged; and the plains, which had always been a major thoroughfare for prehistoric groups from all directions, became a true melting pot. This is especially true of the Panhandle, where a major coalescence of cultures took place, resulting in the first truly sedentary, permanent residents of the plains, known archeologically as the Panhandle Aspect.

Panhandle Aspect

Not truly a tribal name, Panhandle Aspect refers to culturally homogeneous groups who shared many traits and, probably, a common language. Easily the most thoroughly studied and documented culture on the Texas Plains, the Panhandle Aspect people were professionals in the modern sense of the word. They extensively and intensively hunted and processed bison for trade as well as for personal use. They farmed and stored, or perhaps traded, surplus crops, and they mined Alibates agate, establishing trade systems with the Pecos- and Rio Grande-based **Puebloan** groups.

Their structures range from large, **contiguous**-walled complexes to single dwellings. Most are square or rectangular and have eastward-facing entryways. Some interior features include roof-support posts, a west-wall altar or bench, and raised benches along the north and south walls. Centrally placed firepits or hearths are common, as are interior **cache pits**, ash pits, and fireplace **deflectors.** It is the heavy use of stone slabs that differentiates Panhandle Aspect villages from others in the Great Plains. While a few slab-less houses with pole and adobe walls occur, the overwhelming majority of structures have slab-lined, adobe-encased wall foundations or footing walls.

The Panhandle Aspect flourished for some 300 years. During that time, the people opened up many of the quarry pits in what is now the Alibates National Monument and spread Alibates agate far and wide. Their deep trash middens provide direct evidence of the trade. Artifactual materials include at least fifteen known types of Southwestern pottery, as well as flakes and tools of obsidian, pieces of worked turquoise from the west, and Olivella and other marine shell ornaments from the Pacific and Gulf coasts.

Aside from the imported items, Panhandle Aspect artifacts reflect a plains origin and the activities associated with major plains lifeways, such as small, triangular side-notched (Washita) and un-notched (Fresno) bison-hunting arrow points; beveled and double-beveled Harahey knives; grinding slabs; and horticultural tools made from bison *tibiae* and *scapulae.* Panhandle Aspect sites are often recognized by the presence of Borger Cordmarked pottery. Unlike most Woodland ware, which used boiling stones for internal cooking, Borger Cord-marked vessels frequently show exterior charring or blackening from being placed directly into or over fires or beds of coals.

Major reported sites of these people include the Alibates Ruin complex and the Chicken Creek site in Potter County;

Puebloan - coming from the northern Rio Grande pueblos.

contiguous - touching or sharing an edge.

cache pit - a special storage place.

deflector - a slab or stone placed so drafts will be directed away from a hearth.

tibia - the shin bone.

scapula - the large bone that forms the back part of the shoulder.

Washita point

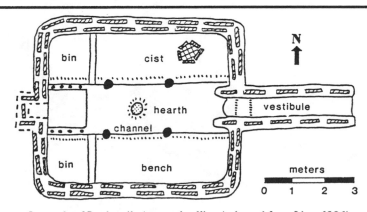

One style of Panhandle Aspect dwelling (adapted from Lintz 1986)

Athapaskan - languages spoken by Navajos and Apaches.

travois - a sled-like carrying device pulled by a dog.

band - a small hunting-gathering society with no status distinctions other than those based on age and sex.

Saddleback Mesa and Landergin Mesa in Oldham County; Cotton-wood and Tarbox Creek ruins and the Blue Creek Ruins complex in Moore County; and the Antelope Creek site and Coetas Ruin in Hutchinson County. Many sites have been lost to, or severely damaged by, the construction and filling of Lake Meredith, oil and gas construction activities, vandalism, and erosion. Of these, vandalism is the most prevalent and most destructive. It is now exceedingly rare to find an intact Panhandle Aspect structure.

Radiocarbon dates for Panhandle Aspect sites indicate that by about A.D. 1450 the culture had almost ceased to function as a coherent group, and many major sites were abandoned by then. Certainly by A.D. 1500 the era of the hunter-farmer-villager had ended, except, perhaps, in the Wolf Creek Valley in Ochiltree and Lipscomb counties. There new studies are revealing that villagers in that area were not "mainstream" Panhandle Aspect peoples, as had long been believed. What happened to these people is unknown, but several theories have been formulated. Soil analyses and other studies strongly suggest that after A.D. 1300 dry spells set in on the High Plains and droughts became more and more frequent. The people may have abandoned their villages and embraced a more nomadic lifestyle. There is also some evidence to suggest that these people joined groups ancestral to the historic Wichitas. There is, however, a human factor proposed for the demise of the peaceful hunter-farmers of the Panhandle—the Apache. Coronado met them in 1541, and they, along with other groups, were by then apparently well established on the High Plains.

HISTORIC PERIOD
(A.D. 1550 to present)

Actually, little is known about the prehistoric Apaches, nor are archeologists sure when the **Athapaskan**-speaking northerners arrived in the Southwest. Certainly, by 1541 the principal occupants of the plains were nomadic bison hunters who lived in hide and skin tepees, transported on **travois** dragged by dogs. For 150 to 200 years, the Apache virtually ruled the plains, as well as much of the Southwest and Texas. Some of the **bands** lived fairly peaceful lives—after dispossessing many other groups, that is. They continued

Dog pulling travois

to use the bow and arrow, often using iron arrow points, a few guns obtained by theft or trade.

micaceous - containing mica.

utilitarian - everyday, practical.

Apache sites are difficult to find or identify. In the Panhandle and other regions, two types of archeological remains are considered suggestive of Apache affiliation: tepee rings and a thin, dark, **micaceous** pottery. Tepee rings are circular clusters of cobbles or slabs, used to hold down the bases of the tepee covers. The pottery is very similar to **utilitarian** pottery from the New Mexican pueblos of Taos and Picuris, where the Apache are known to have traded. They also manufactured arrow points, such as Washita, Fresno, Harrell, and Talco, which other groups used. On the Llano Estacado and in the western Rolling Plains, some Late Prehistoric or early Historic-age sites produce different artifacts that are also thought to be Apache. Point styles recovered from sites in Lubbock and Garza counties often show Puebloan as well as other, ill-defined influences.

The plains, with its large bison herds and other resources, attracted many other groups as changes took place throughout the Southwest. The Comanches in particular were headed toward the southern plains from the north, being pressured by expanding nations, especially the Sioux. By the mid-1700s most Apaches had been driven from the plains and forced to seek shelter and protection among those whom they formerly plundered, the Spanish and the Puebloans.

Supplied with guns and other items by the French and taking horses wherever they found them, the Comanche became the most feared and respected warriors on the Southern Great Plains, where they ruled for over 100 years. Their material remains typically include many European goods, and their burials are especially rich in such materials. Some Comanche sites produce tepee rings and shallow basin hearths devoid of rocks but filled with a fine white or gray ash indicative of buffalo dung fuel. Glass trade beads and metal objects, including points, knives, and gun parts, along with brass or copper trinkets, are common finds with Comanche remains. Burials frequently contain equestrian gear regardless of the age or sex of the deceased, which illustrates the special value placed on the horse by the Comanche, who are considered to have been some of the most highly skilled riders in the world.

During the Comanche reign, other groups appeared on the plains, sharing an uneasy peace with the Indians. The Ciboleros, a colorful group of bison hunters and traders from Mexico and New Mexico, may have impressed the Comanche with their own daring and skills in the hunt. Another group of traders, the Comancheros, appeared on the plains in the mid-1800s or later and ostensibly carried on legitimate trade with Indian groups, obtaining bison hides, leather goods, and meat in exchange for knives, powder and shot, beads, trinkets, and clothing. One interesting site attributed to possible

Fresno point

Cibolero or Comanchero occupation, the Merrell-Taylor site, near Quitaque, contains the remains of three dugouts. Artifacts recovered include a Spanish lance blade and "buffalo" rifles. The site was occupied between about 1865 and 1885, when Comancheros were still active on the plains.

Following the Civil War, Anglo bison hunters began to work their destructive way onto the plains, harvesting thousands of buffalo and driving out the Ciboleros and ultimately the Indians. In late June 1874, several hundred Comanche, Kiowa, and Cheyenne laid siege to Adobe Walls, seeking revenge on this bison-hunter trading post north of the Canadian River. For several days, about 30 Anglos held off the attackers, led by the famous Quanah Parker and a fanatical medicine man named Isatai. When the frustrated Indians pulled back, leaving many dead behind, the Anglos made their way to safety. This battle hastened military action in the region, and in September 1874, Col. Ranald Mackenzie—ironically informed and led by a Comanchero— located a major Comanche camp in Palo Duro Canyon and attacked, destroying the Indians' horse herds, livestock, food supply, and lodges. Without horses and lodges and with winter almost upon them, the Indians were truly defeated and were interned on reservations in Oklahoma. Very soon after, with the bison herds slaughtered and driven north or away from the plains, the New Mexican *pastores*, or sheepherders, were able to bring in their sheep. They built rock and adobe plazas, or settlements, which included rock-walled pens and blinds. Sites of *pastores* have been recorded in several places in the northern Texas plains. The best-known of these is Old Tascosa in Oldham County. This "wild west" frontier town is now the site of Cal Farley's Boys Ranch.

Like so many before them, the *pastores* were not destined to stay long on the plains. Cattlemen, eying the vast grasslands, drove the sheepherders out and became the first truly permanent settlers of the region since the time of the Panhandle Aspect people. To meet the cattle industry's needs, the railroads followed, accompanied by merchants, tradesmen, saloonkeepers, and farmers.

The defeat of the last defiant plains Indian warriors brought to a close a long, complex, colorful era, one that lasted some 12,000 to 15,000 years. It was an era that saw many changes, both in the land and in the many peoples it nurtured.

A new era began in the 1880s, one that promises to be just as complex and fascinating as the previous era. The rich plains continue to support a wide variety of people, many of whom migrated here from other regions, including some newer immigrants from Asia, homeland of the very first visitors to the plains so long ago. Perhaps, as the philosopher said, "The more things change, the more they remain the same."

REFERENCES

Baker, T. Lindsay, and Billy R. Harrison
    1968 *Adobe Walls: The History and Archeology of the 1875 Trading Post.* Panhandle-Plains Historical Museum, Canyon, Texas.

Couzzourt, Jim
    1982 Archeological Testing at Cal Farley's Ranch, Oldham County, Texas. *Transactions of the 17th Regional Archeological Symposium for Southeastern New Mexico and Western Texas.* Southwestern Federation of Archeological Societies. pp. 57-134.

    1988 The Tascosa Creek Site: New Developments and Dates. *Transactions of the 23rd Regional Archeological Symposium for Southeastern New Mexico and Western Texas.* Southwestern Federation of Archeological Societies, pp. 44-79.

Etchieson, Gerald Meeks, and James E. Couzzourt
    1987 *Shoreline Survey at Lake Meredith Recreation Area in the Texas Panhandle.* U.S. Department of the Interior, Bureau of Reclamation, Southwest Region, Amarillo, Texas.

Hughes, David T., and A. Alicia Hughes-Jones
    1987 *The Courson Archeological Projects, Final 1985 and Preliminary 1986 Reports.* Harold D. Courson, Perryton, Texas.

Lintz, Christopher Ray
    1986 *Architecture and Community Variability Within the Antelope Creek Phase of the Texas Panhandle.* Studies in Oklahoma's Past, Number 14. Oklahoma Archeological Survey, Norman, Oklahoma.

Wedel, Waldo R.
    1975 Chalk Hollow: Culture Sequence and Chronology in the Texas Panhandle. In *Actas del 41st Congreso Internacional de Americanistas* 1:270-278. Instituto Nacional de Antropolgia e Historia, Mexico, D.F.

Willey, P.
    1988 The Tascosa Creek Site Skeleton. *Transactions of the 23rd Regional Archeological Symposium for Southeastern New Mexico and Western Texas.* Southwestern Federation of Archeological Societies.

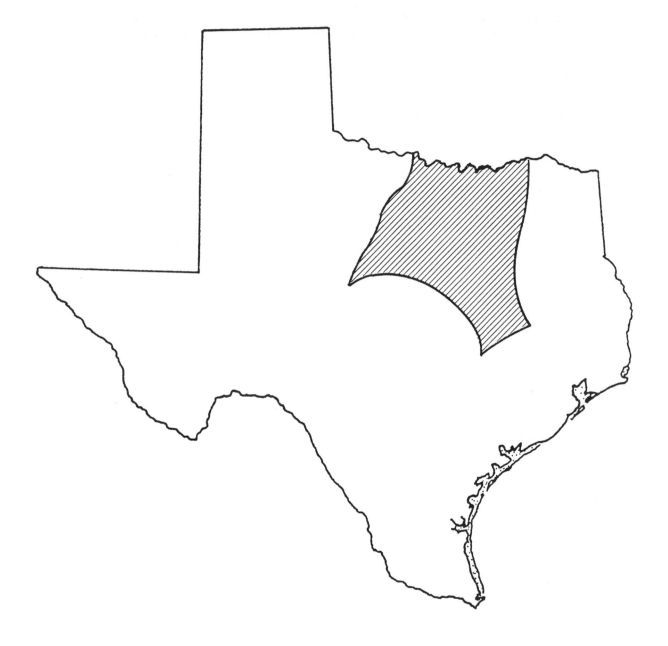

North Central Texas

Cultural Time Periods

LATE PREHISTORIC PERIOD
(A.D. 600 - A.D. 1600)

The Late Prehistoric period in North Central Texas is usually subdivided into early and late periods. The early years from about A.D. 600 to A.D. 1200 are especially significant in the unfolding of the region's prehistory. During this time the bow and arrow and pottery came into use.

Cultural influences from the east and west, from the Caddoan and plains cultural regions, met in North Central Texas. Generally speaking, the early part of the period showed the greatest Caddoan influence. Some researchers have suggested that there was a movement of Caddoan peoples into the eastern sections of the region. As the climate grew warmer around A.D. 1200, the Indians already in the region either adopted typical plains cultural traits; or groups from the plains moved in bringing with them a culture dominated by bison procurement. Whether or not the easterners actually confronted the westerners, coexisted peacefully, or came to blows has yet to be determined, but at sites near Lake Lavon and the city of Waco, burials tell of a violent demise for some of the inhabitants.

With the introduction of the bow and arrow hunting became a more efficient endeavor. Atlatls were still used, since dart points are found along with arrow points in tool **assemblages** dating from the early part of the period. Typical of the generally smaller point types were Scallorn, Rockwall, Catahoula, and Alba. Dog burials, reported in some sites, indicate that domesticated dogs had some significance to these groups, probably as hunting companions.

Ceramic vessels made during the early part of the period were dominated by sand- and **grog-tempered**, utilitarian cooking pots and storage jars. Most of the earliest examples lacked any ornamentation, but later decoration began to copy Caddoan designs, such as **incised** lines, **punctates**, and fingernail impressions.

No one knows precisely when cultivation of maize began, but the presence of quantities of corn at the Cobb-Pool site in southwestern Dallas County has sparked the interest of prehistorians because of the new technology that the discovery represents. The site, located in the West Fork of the Trinity River drainage, was surrounded by a prairie habitat which offered limited resources. Perhaps the people of this area of North Central Texas turned to maize horticulture to round out their subsistence strategy or perhaps they acquired the corn by trade. Gardening required a commitment of time and labor and necessitated a certain degree of **sedentism**. Cobb-Pool seems to have been inhabited at least on a semi-permanent basis, since the inhabitants constructed three houses, platforms for food drying and storage, middens, and a large pit probably used as an earth oven.

assemblage - a collection of artifacts often representing a cultural time period.

grog - crushed pottery used as a tempering material.

temper - material such as crushed bone or shell added to clay before pottery manufacture to reduce shrinkage and breakage during drying and firing.

incised - engraved; cut into with a sharp tool.

punctates - depressions in various shapes and made by various means.

sedentism - the condition of not being mobile or nomadic.

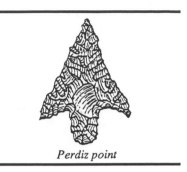

Perdiz point

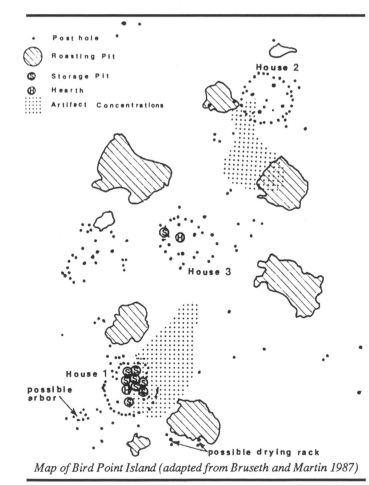

Post hole
Roasting Pit
Storage Pit
Hearth
Artifact Concentrations

House 2

House 3

House 1
possible arbor

possible drying rack

Map of Bird Point Island (adapted from Bruseth and Martin 1987)

Excavation of another hamlet, Bird Point Island, located near Corsicana, provided a slightly different picture of life around A.D. 1100 to 1200. There, three circular structures constructed of wooden posts and thatch sheltered the inhabitants. Maps of artifact distribution compiled by the investigators show work areas for stone-tool manufacture, food processing, cooking, and other activities. By studying these maps archeologists are able to provide interpretations of daily life at the site.

Plant and animal remains found in storage and roasting pits revealed a diversity of diet. Deer, nuts, and a tuber related to the prairie turnip were the staples of life. It is significant to note that unlike the Cobb-Pool site, no evidence of corn was found. Apparently, the immediately accessible natural environment provided Bird Point Islanders with a sufficiently balanced diet without farming.

Around A.D. 1200 changes occurred in pottery and projectile point types, signaling the beginning of the second half of the Late Prehistoric period. The drying-out of the environment produced dynamic cultural changes. Caddoan influence from the east diminished, while cultural ties emanating from the Great Plains and the Texas Plains increased. Bison reappeared on the prairie, possibly in response to the drier climate and wider development of the shortgrasses which they preferred. Artifact assemblages reflect a dispersal of ideas and people from the southern plains. The arrow point types, such as Fresno, Harrell, Washita, and Perdiz, while very different in style, were especially designed to be hafted onto arrow shafts and to bring down bison effectively. Even ceramic technology reflected plains influence in the use of shell as a tempering material; although bone, crushed limestone, and fossil shells were mixed with the clay from time to time.

While bison hunting reigned supreme on the prairies even in these pre-horse days, horticulture was probably becoming a more significant activity. Even gardening, though, made use of the bison. At Lake Lewisville two bison-scapula hoes and a bison-tibia digging stick were found by archeologists. Reports have suggested that horticulture was practiced to some degree on the West Fork of the Trinity, the Red, the Wichita and Little Wichita, and the Central Brazos rivers. These regions provided sandy soil, which was more easily tilled by stone and bone tools than the unyielding prairie clays. Certainly, villages were inhabited on a more permanent basis, making substantial structures and storage pits necessary.

Typical Wichita house

HISTORIC PERIOD (A.D. 1600 - present)

There is great controversy concerning the location and identity of the Indian groups in North Central Texas from the end of Late Prehistoric times to about 1700. Surprisingly, almost less is known about these years than the preceding period. Relatively few early historic sites have been located in spite of careful surveys, although written records document large Indian populations in the area. Questions have been raised surrounding the origin, or homeland, of the Indian groups first contacted by the Spanish in the 1500s. Were these people descendants of the Late Prehistoric groups, or had they recently migrated to North Central Texas? The archeological record appears to indicate a change in cultures brought about by abandonment, reduction in population, or movement of people into the area. It is possible, of course, that combinations of land development, farming, and vandalism have destroyed sites that could supply valuable information on this time period.

The group of Indians known historically as the Wichita was the most widespread in North Central Texas and is the best understood. By the early 1700s they were found from the Red River to the Brazos River. It is known through historical documents that some of them moved south from Kansas under pressure from the Osage and were divided into three principal subgroups. The largest complex of their villages, known as the Spanish Fort site, was probably inhabited by the Taovayas and featured prominently in Spanish and French historical accounts during the 17th century. The Tawakonis and the Wacos had moved farther south and by late 1772 settled on the Brazos River at sites now under Lake Whitney and near the present city of Waco. Other sites of Wichita villages which have been excavated include the Pearson site (now under Lake Tawakoni), the Gilbert site in Rains County, and others in Lamar County on the Red River.

The Wichitas were buffalo-hunting farmers who tilled their fields during three seasons of the year and hunted in winter. When the artist George Catlin visited them in 1832, they were cultivating melons in addition to the usual southwestern fare of corn, beans, and squash. Although they lived near rivers, they seem to have held the typical plains prohibition against eating fish. Structures were durable, grass covered, and round in shape, not too dissimilar from the structures at Bird Point Island 700 years earlier. At the time of first contact with Europeans, the Wichitas were manufacturing their own pottery, but the

intrusive - intruding without permission.

industry seems to have been quickly abandoned in favor of European goods.

Artifacts of native manufacture appear side-by-side with European trade goods in excavated sites. Triangular Fresno points, snub-nosed scrapers, clay and ground-stone pipes, and Caddoan-influenced pottery types are typical. From the Europeans the Wichita had acquired glass trade beads, metal knives, axes, scissors, buttons, guns, kettles, ceramics, and jewelry. The Wichitas practiced their adaptive skills by fashioning metal arrow points from brass and iron, as well as producing cone-shaped tinklers (decorative items) from sheet metal and coins.

Pressure from the western movement of settlers and other Indian groups drove tribes from the eastern United States into Texas during the 1700s and 1800s. Notable among these **intrusive** groups were the Cherokee, Shawnee, Delaware, Kickapoo, Alabama, and Coushatta peoples. The Caddos were displaced from their Northeast Texas home and settled on the Brazos River, either on or very near the site that the Tawakoni had occupied earlier. As land grants were established and more settlers arrived, the Indians of North Central Texas experienced greater anxiety, fear, and unrest. By the end of the Civil War all had been relocated in Oklahoma Indian Territory. Thus ended over 12,000 years of aboriginal culture in North Central Texas.

The archeological record, however, continues with European entry into Texas. According to some historians, it is possible that Moscosa led de Soto's troops across North Central Texas from approximately Texarkana to the Trinity River in 1542. The archeological folklore is full of stories, and even photographs, of Spanish-origin military artifacts. None of these items, unfortunately, has ever been studied in context. Later, settlers carved a niche for themselves by establishing communities and utilizing the abundant resources of the environment. Historical archeologists have studied several of their homesteads and early urban communities. One project in downtown Dallas focused on the residences and yards of several early citizens. Stratigraphy of the site revealed not only 1870s artifacts, but also plow zones from a slightly earlier period overlying prehistoric Indian artifacts.

Our understanding of the prehistory and early history of North Central Texas is enhanced by recognizing the important relationship of the people to the land. Each microenvironment produced its unique set of resources, constraints,

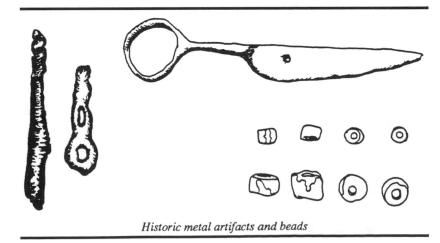

Historic metal artifacts and beads

and requisite adaptations. The aboriginal people, early explorers, and settlers were creative and flexible survivors, each group utilizing in its own way the diverse offerings of the land.

REFERENCES

Bruseth, James, and William Martin
  1987 Prehistoric Settlement at Bird Point Island. In *Bird Point Island and Adams Ranch Sites: Methodological and Theoretical Contributions to North Central Texas Archaeology*. Edited by James Bruseth and William Martin. Richland Technical Series, Vol. 2, Archaeology Research Program, Southern Methodist University, Dallas, Texas.

Catlin, George
  1973 *Letters and Notes on the Manners, Customs, and Conditions of North American Indians*, Vol. 2. Dover Publications, New York.

Ferring, C. Reid
  1986 Late Quaternary Geology and Environments of the Upper Trinity Basin. In *An Assessment of the Cultural Resources in the Trinity River Basin, Dallas, Tarrant, and Denton Counties, Texas*. Edited by Bonnie C. Yates and C. Reid Ferring. Institute of Applied Sciences, University of North Texas, Denton, Texas.

Fox, Daniel E.
  1983 *Traces of Texas History: Archeological Evidence of the Past 450 Years*. Corona Publishing Co., San Antonio, Texas.

Lynott, Mark
  1977 *A Regional Model for Archeological Research in Northcentral Texas*. Ph.D. dissertation. Southern Methodist University, Dallas, Texas.

  1981 A Model of Prehistoric Adaptation in Northern Texas. *Plains Anthropologist* 26(92)97-100.

Moir, Randall, Duane Peter, David Jurney, and Daniel McGregor
  1988 *Archaeological and Historical Investigations of Joe Pool Lake, North Central Texas*. Archaeology Research Program, Southern Methodist University, Dallas, Texas.

Newcomb, W.W., Jr.
  1961 *The Indians of Texas from Prehistoric to Modern Times*. University of Texas Press, Austin, Texas.

Prikryl, Daniel
  1987 *A Synthesis of Prehistory of the Lower Elm Fork of the Trinity River*. Masters thesis, University of Texas at Austin, Austin, Texas.

Skinner, S. Alan
  1988 Where Did All the Indians Go? *The Record* 42(3)101-106. Dallas Archeological Society, Dallas, Texas.

Stephenson, Robert
  1970 Archeological Investigations in the Whitney Reservoir Area, Central Texas. *Bulletin of the Texas Archeological Society*. Vol. 41.

Central Texas

Cultural Time Periods

LATE PREHISTORIC PERIOD
(A.D. 600 or 700 - 1600)

chronological markers artifacts from a certain time period which are judged to represent a change in culture.

The beginning of the Late Prehistoric period, about A.D. 600, is heralded by the introduction of the bow and arrow and ceramics. The new weapon necessitated significant changes in stone-tool types, and small arrow points of distinctive styles are found in sites dating to this period. In Central Texas the Scallorn arrow point early in the Late Prehistoric (Austin Phase) and the Perdiz point later (Toyah Phase) are good **chronological markers**. More than likely the Indians did not totally abandon the use of the spear and atlatl, but with the bow and arrow added a significant new weapon to their inventory.

Comparisons of the Austin and Toyah phases reveal certain differences in lifestyle of the Central Texas people. One study based on radiocarbon dates suggests that progressive waves of cultural change moved from north to south throughout the Late Prehistoric period and into the Historic period. This pattern of change closely parallels developments which took place on the Texas plains and in the North Central Texas region and was triggered by environmental changes as well as the movement of people and ideas.

The Austin Phase Indians depended slightly more on gathered foods than on hunting. Their sites reveal freshwater mussels were consumed, and the shells were fashioned into beads and pendants. Burial practices included a significant use of cemeteries containing both cremated and noncremated remains.

During the latter half of the Late Prehistoric, or Toyah Phase, hunting increased in importance. The bison herds returned and, based on the numbers of butchered bison bones and bone tools found in sites, the animal played an important role in the Indians' life. At large village sites, such as Rowe Valley in Williamson County, animal-processing areas are clearly delineated and often located downwind from the site.

Pottery was present during the Toyah Phase even though the hunting-gathering lifeway persisted. Some pottery was manufactured in Central Texas, but numerous sites in the region yield vessel fragments that bear traits of East Texas Caddoan ware. The Toyah people may have traded for the Caddoan pottery or simply borrowed Caddoan techniques; some may have acquired Caddo wives, who brought pots with them or made them in Central Texas; or, perhaps, Caddoan settlement pushed westward into Central Texas. Regardless of how the vessels arrived in Central Texas, it is interesting that mobile populations moving on foot would be transporting fragile pottery.

Central Texas inhabitants possibly established more permanent settlements during the second half of the Late Prehistoric period. Isolated corncob finds at some sites suggest limited horticultural activities, but trade with Caddoan or other sedentary groups could also

Scallorn point

Perdiz point

protohistoric - period of time just before recorded history.

Americam bison

explain the presence of corn. Research in the future will hopefully shed light on this issue. A few sites which have already yielded information on the Late Prehistoric period are the Kyle site in Hill County, Finis Frost in San Saba County, and Landslide in Bell County.

HISTORIC PERIOD (A.D. 1600 - present)

By the seventeenth century, European explorers had made contact with Central Texas native inhabitants and had begun to influence their cultural traditions with the introduction of European-produced goods. Artifacts such as glass beads and metal tools found at Indian sites are indicative of European contact and date a site to sometime after A.D. 1500. By the mid-eighteenth century, the original Indian populations found by the Europeans in Central Texas had been pushed into marginal areas by intrusive groups. The Apaches swept down from the plains during the 1600s and early 1700s, and the Comanches followed by the mid-1700s.

It is very difficult to identify specific historic Indian groups from their sites, since items of European manufacture exist side-by-side with typical Late Prehistoric artifacts. Spanish Colonial mission records often document the Indians whom the Spanish sought to convert. During the mid-eighteenth century, the historic Tonkawas joined other Texas Indians in seeking protection at Spanish missions which were located primarily in neighboring regions. The Tonkawa population was being decimated by conflict with other Indian groups intruding into Tonkawan territory and by European diseases. In 1859 the surviving Tonkawas were removed to Oklahoma Indian Territory. A few individuals were employed as scouts for the U.S. Cavalry during the 1870s.

The origin of the ancestral groups of the Tonkawa is obscure. Drastic changes in cultural patterns during the early Historic period make it difficult to interpret the archeological record and distinguish between Late Prehistoric groups and their descendants who were in contact with Europeans. Few archeological sites have been recognized as historic Tonkawan; however, recent excavations by members of the Texas Archeological Society near Rowe Valley in Williamson County have revealed evidence of **protohistoric** Indian occupation. Tools and archeological features at the Rowe Valley site are typical of numerous Central Texas prehistoric sites. In addition, the occurrence of artifacts datable to the time period of A.D. 1650 to 1750 could link occupation of the site to the nearby San Xavier missions that were established for the Tonkawas in 1748 and 1749.

Early structures connected with the Anglo-American settlement of Texas have been the object of historical archeology projects in Central Texas. At McKinney Falls State Park, the 1850s homestead complex built by Thomas F. McKinney originally featured a mill, horse-training facilities, and several other structures. After an initial survey, excavation further revealed the functions of various buildings and yard areas of the complex. Urban archeology has not been neglected in Central Texas. The city of Austin has witnessed many projects including excavations at the French Legation, the Carrington-Covert House, the 1853 Capitol, the temporary Capitol of 1883-1888, and several other historic structures now used as offices or businesses.

Compared to the whole picture of past human lifeways in Central Texas, only a few puzzle pieces remain. Through archeological investigations, prehistory and history have been clarified and immeasurably enriched. Future scientific investigations will no doubt add to our knowledge, as long as cultural resources are preserved and protected from destruction.

REFERENCES

Fox, Daniel E.
  1983   *Traces of Texas History: Archeological Evidence of the Past 450 Years.* Corona Publishing Company, San Antonio, Texas.

Fox, Daniel E. (editor)
  1988   *Aboriginal Central Texas: Cultural Patterning of an Environmentally Transitional Region.* Manuscript on file with the Department of Anthropology, Baylor University, Waco, Texas.

Newcomb, W.W., Jr.
  1961   *The Indians of Texas: from Prehistoric to Modern Times.* University of Texas Press, Austin, Texas.

Prewitt, Elton R.
  1981   Cultural Chronology of Central Texas. *Bulletin of the Texas Archeological Society* 52:65-89.
  1983   From Circleville to Toyah: Comments on Central Texas Chronology. *Bulletin of the Texas Archeological Society* 54:201-238.

Roberson, Wayne R.
  1974   *The Carrington-Covert House.* Office of the State Archeologist, Report #25, Texas Historical Commission, Austin, Texas.

Suhm, Dee Ann
  1960   A Review of Central Texas Archeology. *Bulletin of the Texas Archeological Society* 29:63-107.

Turner, Ellen Sue, and Thomas R. Hester
  1985   *A Field Guide to Stone Artifacts of Texas Indians.* Texas Monthly Press, Austin, Texas.

Northeast Texas

Cultural Time Periods

EARLY CERAMIC PERIOD (200 B.C. - A.D. 700)

The Early Ceramic period in Northeast Texas represents the earliest break from the long-entrenched Archaic tradition in Texas. Two major cultural events occurred during this time period; first was the introduction of ceramics, followed by the bow and arrow. Emphasizing that the use of pottery developed within the region, Harry Shafer has written:

> The widespread popularity of the Gary [point type] assemblages in both time and space serves as a good indication that the introduction of ceramics was not made by populations with different technology invading the area. The adoption of ceramic technology was made by indigenous populations and had no apparent affect on either the settlement pattern or stone technology.

The first pottery in the southern and central part of eastern Texas was a sandy-paste (nontempered) ware. In Northeast Texas the early pottery is usually identified as Williams Plain, a bone- or grog-tempered, undecorated ware. The differences between these two pottery types are discrete and not explainable by variations in clays. They seem to represent two different cultural traditions. Pottery from both areas was of simple utilitarian function, that is, simple bowls and jars. Decoration occurred rarely on the sandy-paste wares, but when it did occur, the designs were incised or punctate patterns or combinations of both.

An interesting event of this period was an extension of the **Marksville** culture into western Louisiana and eastern Texas. This is illustrated by the Jonas Short and Coral Snake mounds in the Sam Rayburn and Toledo Bend Lake areas. The mounds included cremation burials as well as **exotic** trade items, such as copper bracelets, copper ear ornaments, copper beads, and **boatstones**, as well as large flint knives. A time period between 100 B.C. and A.D. 400 is attributed to this culture in Northeast Texas. The presence of a trade network to obtain copper artifacts from either the Great Lakes area or from Georgia and the ability to control labor for a project as arduous as mound construction imply a social organization of some complexity.

During the Early Ceramic period, pottery appeared with the Gary-Kent Archaic dart point assemblage. Corner-notched arrow points joined this assemblage later than did the pottery.

LATE PREHISTORIC PERIOD (A.D. 700 - 1700)

The Late Prehistoric period in Northeast Texas is synonymous with the Caddo Indians and their mound sites. Research has not shown a

Marksville - a culture of the Lower Mississippi Valley.

exotic - unusual or rare for that culture; often acquired by trade.

boatstone - a canoe-shaped ground stone artifact which may have been used as a atlatl weight.

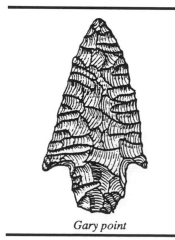

Gary point

retainer - a servant or attendant.

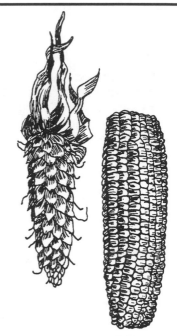

Early variety of maize (left) compared to modern corn (right)

slow evolution of the Caddo from the indigenous people, except possibly in the great bend of the Red River. The early part of the period is marked by major village and mound sites, maize (corn) agriculture, and high-status burials, with exotic burial goods and sometimes **retainers** interred with the principal party. These sites were not numerous but, as major centers, probably interacted with and influenced outlying communities.

The use of the bow and arrow, which began during Early Ceramic times, continued throughout the Late Prehistoric period. The use of the atlatl and Gary dart points, which survive from the earlier weapon system, may also have been carried over, but this has not been archeologically proven.

The introduction of maize, a major food source, allowed most Caddoan groups to live in one site the year round and to give up the previous nomadic lifestyle, which had carried them from one food source to another as the seasons changed.

With the sedentary way of life, the production of pottery vessels increased in quantity, quality, and style. Like the changes in dart point shape and style, which are used as markers to establish contemporaneity of the earlier people, pottery vessels having similar shapes and design motifs have been named and are used by archeologists to serve as time markers in the Caddo, or Late Prehistoric, time period. These designs changed with time and with the locale in which they were produced.

One of the best known of the early Caddo mound sites associated with a large village is the George C. Davis site located on the Neches River in Cherokee County. Excavation of the site was begun in the 1930s as a part of a WPA project and continued in the late 1960s and early 1970s under the direction of Dee Ann Story of the University of Texas at Austin. To date it is probably the most important site excavated in Northeast Texas. It is now incorporated into Caddo Mounds State Park and features an excellent interpretive center.

Large civic-ceremonial centers like the Davis site contained some special-use structures which were periodically destroyed, covered by earth, and rebuilt on the newly raised mound. Cemetery mounds were also enlarged when needed. The large Northeast Texas sites served as regional distribution and exchange centers for a complex social system. The artifacts

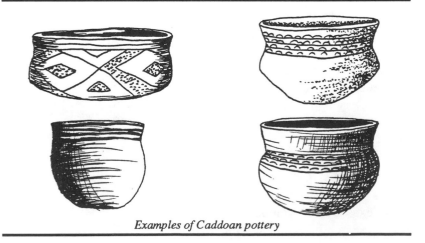

Examples of Caddoan pottery

recovered provide a picture of sociopolitical complexity and demand for exotic, luxurious goods.

Washington Square in downtown Nacogdoches, the Sanders site in Lamar County, and the Hatchel Mound northwest of Texarkana are other examples of early mound sites. The Hatchel site is akin to several nearby mound sites in the southwest corner of Arkansas.

The latter part of the Late Prehistoric period is characterized by village sites, which in several cases contain one to three small mounds. These mounds appear to have been built over the remains of a structure, but unlike most habitational sites, the usual accumulation of trash is missing. Possibly, all debris of the house had been removed before the mound was constructed over it. This mound-over-structure trait appears to be a carry-over from the large mound center tradition.

The Late Prehistoric time period is best known from the cemetery sites. The dead were usually interred with three to fifteen pottery vessels. Sometimes **celts** and arrow points and, occasionally, a pipe were included.

HISTORIC PERIOD (A.D. 1550 - present)

The region that is now Northeast Texas, and the Indians that occupied it, were first known to Europeans when the De Soto expedition under the direction of Moscosa entered the area in 1542 during their aborted attempt to reach Mexico by land. Historians report that in the 1600s, most of the aboriginal people were in three or four loose confederations. The largest group, the Hasinai, occupied parts of what is now Nacogdoches, Rusk, Cherokee, and Houston counties. The Kadohadachoes, or Caddo proper, were at the bend of the Red River above Texarkana. A third group was situated where the present city of Natchitoches, Louisiana, is located. A fourth tribe was on the Red River between the Natchitoches group and the Kadohadachoes.

The attempt by the Spanish to establish missions in the 1690s within the Hasinai area began the period of early and fairly regular written accounts. These missions failed, but others were established in 1716. For the next century the Caddoes struggled to survive peacefully in their homeland in spite of European-introduced disease.

The archeological record shows that as early as 1600 European trade goods from Mexico were reaching the Caddoes of Northeast Texas. These items usually are found in Caddoan graves and consist of Venetian glass beads and, occasionally, iron objects. As time passed the quantity of European trade items increased in the Indian settlements.

In 1719 a Frenchman, Bernard de la Harpe, canoed up the Red and Sulphur rivers with the intent of establishing a trading post in Northeast Texas. From the Sulphur River he journeyed northeast to a

Caddoan effigy pipe
(drawn from Turner and Hester 1985)

Kaddohadacho village, where he was apparently well received by the Indians. He established the Nassonite post near the village, which was occupied by both French and Indians until 1778.

Research and excavation in the 1960s and 1970s located the probable site of the trading post. Known as the Rosebrough Lake site, the area of careful excavation yielded artifacts of both Indian and European manufacture. Several types of Caddoan pottery, clay pipes, and arrow points were found along with sherds of French, Spanish, and British ceramics. Glass artifacts included bottle fragments and mirrors, while all kinds of metal objects ranging from horse-bridle pieces to scissors were recovered.

After the Louisiana Purchase settlers of several nationalities and many ethnic backgrounds streamed steadily into Northeast Texas. Some came legally as citizens of Spain and later Mexico, and others came as illegals. No matter what the means, by 1830 there were more Anglo-Americans in Texas than Mexican nationals and Indians combined. In addition, displaced Indians from the east entered the state and settled in present-day Smith, Cherokee, and surrounding counties. These immigrants included Shawnees, Delawares, Kickapoos, Seminoles, and Cherokees. The inevitable conflicts between these groups led to several attempts to conclude a treaty, but it was not until 1843 that one was signed between the Republic of Texas and several of the Indian tribes. It was by this treaty that the early inhabitants of East Texas lost the land which their ancestors had inhabited for thousands of years.

Historic period bottles

REFERENCES

Davis, E. Mott
    1970   Archeological and Historical Assessment of the Red River Basin in Texas. In *Archeological and Historical Resources of the Red River Basin*, edited by Hester A. Davis. Arkansas Archeological Survey, Research Series, No.1, Fayetteville, Arkansas.

Fox, Daniel E.
    1983   *Traces of Texas History: Archeological Evidence of the Past 450 Years*. Corona Publishing Company, San Antonio, Texas.

Shafer, Harry J.
    1973   *Lithic Technology at the George C. Davis Site, Cherokee County, Texas*. Ph.D. dissertation. The University of Texas at Austin, Austin, Texas.

    1975   Comments on Woodland Cultures of East Texas. *Bulletin of the Texas Archeological Society* 46:249-254.

Story, Dee Ann
    1981   An Overview of the Archeology of East Texas. *Plains Anthropologist* 26:139-156.

Suhm, Dee Ann, Alex D. Krieger, and Edward B. Jelks
    1954   An Introductory Handbook of Texas Archeology. *Bulletin of the Texas Archeological Society* Vol. 25.

Swanton, John R.
    1942   *Source Material on the History and Ethnology of the Caddo Indians*. Bureau of American Ethnology, Bulletin No.132, Washington, D.C.

Thurmond, J. Peter
    1985   Late Caddoan Social Group Identifications and Sociopolitical Organization in the Upper Cypress Basin and Northeastern Texas. *Bulletin of the Texas Archeological Society* 54:185-200.

Turner, Robert L. Jr.
    1978   The Tuck Carpenter Site and Its Relation to Other Sites Within the Titus Focus. *Bulletin of the Texas Archeological Society* 49:1-110.

Southeast Texas

Cultural Time Periods

EARLY CERAMIC PERIOD (A.D.100-800)

The Early Ceramic period in Southeast Texas begins around A.D.100 with the first use of pottery vessels, the introduction of the bow and arrow, and the possible use of fish **weirs** in tidal areas. Ceramic technology spread from east to west along the coast over a period of several hundreds of years. As might be expected from the direction of the movement, there was an important influence in ideas and technology coming from the Lower Mississippi Valley. The earliest pottery recovered from archeological sites is untempered. Later, sand, grog, bone, and shell provided the tempering material.

The development of the bow and arrow and fish weirs constituted more efficient ways of procuring food, as well as a shift to utilizing a greater variety of species and smaller prey. Fish weirs were fashioned from brush and used to block tidal streams, so that fish could be more easily caught or speared.

The population of both coastal and inland Indian groups increased during the Early Ceramic period. The archeological record shows that the number of villages located near water sources and shellfish resources doubled, and cemeteries appeared for the first time. As in other areas the presence of cemeteries served as possible territorial markers.

LATE PREHISTORIC PERIOD (A.D. 800-1700)

The Late Prehistoric period is characterized by new decorative ceramic styles, greater use of the bow and arrow, and increased population along the coast. With the exception of an early stage, the sequence of ceramic development is similar for the Galveston Bay, the lower Brazos River, and Conroe-Livingston areas. Certain styles appear more frequently around Galveston Bay, but that area has been the subject of intense investigation, thereby yielding more artifacts. As might be expected from the geography, there is a greater occurrence of Caddoan pottery in the Conroe-Livingston area.

Stone tools manufactured during the Late Prehistoric period show little variation from area to area. Most of the raw material was obtained from local sources and included **chert**, quartzite, and petrified wood. Only in the Brazos Delta was chert used almost exclusively. It has been suggested that the **gastroliths** of alligators and large birds also provided raw material for arrow points, especially around Galveston Bay.

Other materials also were used in tools pro-

weir - a barrier placed in a stream to catch fish.

chert - a stone formed in limestone; widely used in making prehistoric tools.

gastrolith - a small, stony mass formed in the stomach.

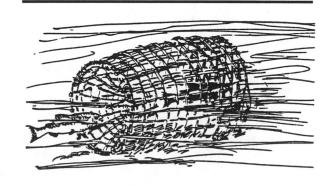

Example of fish weir

seasonal rounds - the trips made to obtain food resources in season.

duction. Bone tools are widely found in Southeast Texas. Beginning in the Early Ceramic period and continuing into the Late Prehistoric period, socketed-bone projectile points are recovered from sites along the coast. Some of these points have blunt ends, presumably designed so that the body of the prey would not be damaged. As a result, feathers destined for trade or ceremonies could be obtained in good condition.

Besides bird, fish, and alligator, many animals both large and small made up the Indians' diet. Along the coast the inhabitants profited from both marine and terrestrial resources. Probably the best-known archeological landmarks are the shell middens. These deposits of clam and oyster shells not only serve as site indicators, but also are often useful in dating archeological deposits. The usual method of dating wood charcoal is rarely possible in the region, since natural vegetation of the coastal areas in prehistoric times was mostly grasses and shrubs which left little datable remains. Shell, however, in the form of *Rangia cuneata*, a brackish water clam, is plentiful, and in spite of difficulties, it has been helpful as a material for radiocarbon dating techniques.

While a hunting-gathering lifestyle continued into the Historic period, there are seasonal campsites which indicate significant reuse over a long period of time. The inland coastal-plain Indian groups were highly mobile in Late Prehistoric times and established campsites near water sources. The coastal margin inhabitants appear to have been more sedentary, spending time at the shell midden sites during the summer and moving slightly inland during the winter months. There seems to have been a greater concentration of people in the coastal areas, probably because of the diversity of resources. It has been estimated that by the end of the Late Prehistoric period villages along the coast housed as many as 400 to 500 people.

HISTORIC PERIOD (A.D. 1500 - present)

In about 1529, Cabeza de Vaca became the first European to set foot in Texas. The chronicle of his trip painted an ecological and ethnographic picture of the Indians in the coastal area as he saw and interpreted it. Much of the archeological data from the preceding period can be more fully understood in light of this valuable picture.

Cabeza de Vaca detailed the **seasonal rounds** by which the Indians gathered the resources of the land, since none of the ecological zones were capable of supporting the people for an entire year. During the months of October through February women along the coast dug underwater roots and took fish in cane traps. The fall pecan harvest provided an additional source of protein to the diet. Blackberries were harvested in April and May, while during the summer months of June and July the coastal Indians moved inland to harvest the fruit of the

Prickly pear cactus

prickly pear. During some winter periods oysters and water were the only sustenance. Women seemed to be responsible for the gathering or harvesting, and De Vaca noted that the women toiled incessantly. In spite of all this work, it is possible that bands of coastal Indians assembled when surpluses were available to share in the harvest and other social events. Coastal villages were temporary, and shelter consisted of huts made of mats. The structures were sometimes large and open with multiple interior hearths. Floors were covered with oyster shells, and animal skins were put down for bedding. Reflecting the temperate climate, men wore no clothing and women wore Spanish moss or deerskin. Body decoration was practiced, and cane was used to pierce the males' ears, nipples, and lower lips.

Sharing and redistribution of resources seem to have been the rule. A host was expected to be generous with his guests. After marriage, a daughter took all of her husband's game to her father's house, and in return the father provided for the couple. Sons were forbidden to communicate with their in-laws. In theory, at least, this solved the problem of disagreement over redistribution.

The shaman, or medicine man, was viewed as a unique individual. This attitude may have provided a social solution for outcasts and misfits. At the strong encouragement of the Indians, De Vaca, himself, became a medicine man, which probably made it easier for them to accept him into their band. The shaman was consulted as a healer and maintained different marriage and funeral practices from the rest of the band. Although religious practices are not entirely understood, the idea of limited **animism** is reflected in their feeling that stones contained power. Sorcery, also, seems to have been a source of great strength.

Trade was carried on by De Vaca between the coast and the northern interior. Being a neutral party, he had considerable access to the interior of the region. From the coast he selected sea snails, conch shells, sea beads, and some form of adhesive for trade with interior groups. In return the inland people sent skins, **red ocher**, hard canes for arrows, flint, sinews, tassels of deer hair, and mesquite beans to the coast.

As in other regions of the state scholars have debated the identity and location of various Indian groups around the time of European contact. It is now recognized that in Southeast Texas there were four major groups, the Atakapas, the Akokisas, the Bidais, and the Karankawas. This latter group represented several tribes who spoke dialects of the same language and were closely related by marriage. The majority of Indians in the region, however, were Atapakan speakers. Territorial divisions for the early eighteenth century have been proposed based on several ethnographic sources. The Atakapas claimed an area which extended from Louisiana across the Sabine River to a line west of Beaumont. The Akokisa were found in a wide area around Galveston

animism - a belief in which natural phenomena and animate and inanimate things are thought to possess a soul.

red ocher - iron oxide mixed with sand and clay and used as a coloring pigment, often ceremonially.

Bay north to Conroe, while the Bidais were in the vicinity of Huntsville. A long, narrow, coastal territory running west of Galveston and extending into South Texas was claimed by the Karankawas.

Much controversy surrounds the historic Karankawas. It has been suggested that this group may be the most maligned of all the Indians in Texas. There is no archeological evidence that the Karankawas living along the upper Texas coast were cannibals, although ritual cannibalism was not unusual among Indian groups in North America. On the contrary Thomas Hester feels that "it was the Karankawa who were shocked by the sight of the starving Spaniards of the Navarez expedition eating the dead of their own party." Historian W.W. Newcomb observed the following:

> Some of the atrocities attributed to these Indians are undoubtedly rationalizations growing out of the inhuman, unfair treatment the Spaniards and Texans accorded them. It is much easier to slaughter men and appropriate their land if you can convince yourself that they are despicable, inferior, barely human creatures.

It is possible that the Spaniards may have intentionally spread the rumor of Indian cannibalism to scare foreign competition away from the Texas coast.

Archeological excavations by the universities and avocational archeological societies in the region are adding to the knowledge of early Euro-American history along the upper Texas coast. The Brazos

Plantation community (drawn from Silverthorne 1986)

River was an important highway in early Texas, and the rich flood plains supported Texas' largest **antebellum** plantations. Research at these sites is presenting a new and different explanation of plantation life in Texas. In addition, archeological investigations on Galveston Island and in downtown Houston at the Brown Convention Center and on Old Market Square have revealed new information about early urban life. Historic archeology not only retrieves information that has gone unrecorded, it also provides the science of archeology with the opportunity to test theories of behavior.

antebellum - before the Civil War (pre 1861).

REFERENCES

Aten, Lawrence E.
    1983 *Indians of the Upper Texas Coast*. Academic Press, New York.

Covey, Cyclone (translator and editor)
    1983 *Cabeza de Vaca's Adventures in the Unknown Interior of America*. University of New Mexico Press, Albuquerque, New Mexico.

Hester, Thomas R.
    1980 *Digging Into South Texas Prehistory, A Guide for Amateur Archaeologists*. Corona Publishing Company, San Antonio, Texas.

Newcomb, W.W. Jr.
    1961 *The Indians of Texas: From Prehistoric to Modern Times*. University of Texas Press, Austin, Texas.

Silverthorne, Elizabeth
    1986 *Plantation Life in Texas*. Texas A &M University Press, College Station, Texas.

Story, Dee Ann
    1985 Adaptive Strageties of Archaic Cultures of the West Gulf Coastal Plain. In *Prehistoric Food Production in North America*, edited by R.J. Ford, Museum of Anthropology, University of Michigan, Anthropological Papers No. 25, pp. 19-56. Ann Arbor, Michigan.

Wheat, Patricia, and Richard L. Gregg (editors)
    1988 *A Collection of Papers Reviewing the Archeology of Southeast Texas*. Houston Archeology Society, Report No. 5. Houston, Texas.

South Texas

Cultural Time Periods

LATE PREHISTORIC PERIOD (A.D. 800-1500)

The introduction of the bow and arrow marks the beginning of the Late Prehistoric period in the South Texas region. The presence of this new weapon seems to have occurred somewhat later here than in northern parts of the state. A typical tool kit of this time consisted of arrow points, small end scrapers, and beveled knives. These tools were associated with killing and processing animals, which strongly suggest a change in culture. The southerly movement of bison herds seen throughout Texas from the middle of the Late Prehistoric period also influenced technology in the region. At a bison-kill site, known as Skillet Mountain and located in the Choke Canyon Resevoir basin, remains from the slaughtered animals were found mixed with several stone tool types.

Pottery of this time period was characterized by **unslipped** containers, mainly *ollas*, having a sandy paste or bone tempering. These vessels were sometimes decorated with asphaltum, red pigment, or incising. A few ceramic figures also have been found in sites, along with smoking pipes, shell ornaments, and bone tools and ornaments.

The environmental conditions of the Late Prehistoric period were considerably different than those of today. Studies have revealed that significant differences between the two periods exist in vegetation patterns, availability of water, and kinds of animals present. Formerly, a savannah grassland covered much of the region, and the streams of major drainages and their tributaries flowed perennially. The overgrazing of cattle and deep-well irrigation are some of the factors which have contributed to present environmental conditions. Bison, antelope, and prairie dog once inhabited South Texas, while certain species such as quail, armadillo, and javelina have appeared in modern times. Along the coast in the Grullo and Baffin bays, native oysters were once enjoyed by prehistoric Indians but are not available to residents today.

Based on information from archeological studies, the Late Prehistoric Indians of South Texas followed two basic patterns of adaptation to their environment. Along the coast a **littoral** lifestyle exploited the resources of the Gulf, lagoons, bays, and offshore islands to the fullest. These people also utilized the ajoining grasslands and forest zones. Given the proximity of these various resource areas, it is possible that the people remained closer to home in their day-to-day or seasonal travels than did the inhabitants of the interior.

Some raw materials, such as stone suitable for tool making, were not immediately available along the coast. The scarcity of stone, however, was balanced by the abundance of shell. Conch and clam shells were fashioned into tools as well as ornaments. Shell middens have been recognized for years as indicators of past habitation. Cabeza

unslipped - without a clay and water solution applied to add color or make a smooth surface.

littoral - relating to a shore or coastal region.

de Vaca noted that often these prehistoric trash disposal areas formed the foundations of houses.

Around Corpus Christi, Grullo, and Baffin bays, and in the Brownsville area, the Indians developed lifeways which were typical of the littoral adaptation. The Late Prehistoric people of the Corpus Christi area utilized shell of the sunray clam for production of utilitarian scrapers, points, and knives. The stone usually available for tool-making was so scarce that only the most efficient production techniques were utilized in the manufacturing process. Very little material was wasted.

Farther down the coast, the Indians around Brownsville probably participated in an active trade network which reached deep into Mexico. There seems to have been a massive shell industry, with production geared toward ornaments. Many Mesoamerican artifacts have been found in the area, and their presence leads researchers to speculate about an exchange network of goods.

The second basic pattern of human adaptation found in South Texas developed in the inland regions. Both the grasslands and forests of this large area served as prehistoric supermarkets for the daily needs of the aboriginal people. The most desirable campsite location was close to the resources of both the floodplain and the forest. Sources of stone for tools and hearths was important. Often terraces in these inland areas contained gravel from which tool-producing cobbles could be obtained. Several sites in Zavala County along the Chaparrosa and Turkey creeks are examples of sites which take advantage of all possible resources.

Choke Canyon on the lower Frio River also was home to groups who exploited the resources close at hand. Archeological work completed there seems to indicate reuse of campsites over a long period of time by people who traveled within limited territories. There must have been a great diversity of diet, judging from the recovered animal remains, such as snake, turtle, jackrabbit, cottontail rabbit, squirrel, catfish, bison, deer, and antelope. The abundant resources favored a gathering of bands on a seasonal basis in historic times, so group harvesting of pecans, acorns, and fruit of the prickly pear probably occurred in Late Prehistoric times also.

In contrast to the intensely used sites, there are campsites which appear to have been occupied for only short periods. Such campsites were located near temporary water sources and seem to have been used only sporadically. Fluctuations in climate and availability of food caused these people to be highly mobile. The inhabitants continually searched for resources and in some cases probably had to dig in stream beds to obtain water. Certain sites in Zavala, Jim Wells, and Starr counties exhibit typical short-use traits exemplified by a few diverse tool types located around a hearth or cooking area.

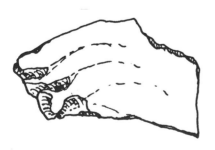

Example of shell scraper

HISTORIC PERIOD (A.D. 1500 - present)

Historic Era Indian Groups

Our knowledge of South Texas Indian groups of the historic era is largely limited to incidental encounters reported by Spanish chroniclers and occasional accounts given by early travelers and settlers. Archival research along with the scant archeological remains have been used to piece together fragments of information known about native Texans of this period.

Numerous small, dispersed groups of hunting, fishing, and gathering Indians were reported by Cabeza de Vaca during his journey through South Texas and northern Mexico. His reports offer some of the best information on the Indians of the region. It is often difficult, however, to distinguish the specific locale and identity of the groups being cited.

Each small Indian band or group was apparently based on an extended family unit; these groups gathered into larger ones for communal collection of seasonal foodstuffs or for shared ceremonies or hunts. Although the inland landscape was not a bountiful one, thick concentrations of certain resources, especially the prickly pear, the **maguey**, and mesquite bean pods, were present. Seasonal availability of these resources and such foods as pecans, acorns, berries, other succulents, seeds, deer, and bison dictated where and when the Indian groups moved and camped. Items used by them included the bow and arrow, the rabbit stick, nets for hunting and fishing, manos and metates, gourds, and, for some of the groups, pottery. Temporary shelters were constructed of brush or hide.

Historic Indians of South Texas have traditionally been divided into two general groups: the inland Coahuiltecan-speaking peoples, and the Karankawa, who depended on coastal resources for their livelihood. This is a generalization, however, and does not allow for the diversity of cultures that may have been present. Indeed, certain peoples, such as the Mariames, alternated between inland and coastal areas. During the eighteenth and nineteenth centuries, Comanches and Apaches made forays into the area, adding to the cultural variety.

Remains of Historic period Indians are occasionally identified through the discovery of glass trade beads or metal points, which are cut from European-style implements such as pots or pans. These kinds of artifacts are not linked to any particular Indian group. Most archeological data derived from historic-era Indians are based on work conducted at various mission complexes, and a "mission" arrow point (sometimes called Guerrero) is frequently discovered in this context. Drastic change began to disrupt the ancient lifeways of the aboriginal

maguey - the century plant

Mesquite with bean pods

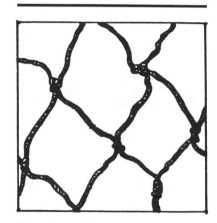

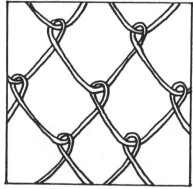
Examples of nets

presidio - a garrison established by the Spanish.

palisaded - a tall fence forming a defensive barrier.

Texans with the arrival of the Europeans, who brought with them new technology, the horse, and disease.

European, Mexican, and Anglo Presence

Traces of early Spanish occupation are found in mission sites and have also been discovered offshore in Spanish shipwrecks. Off the coast of Padre Island, a flotilla of ships sailing toward Havana was lost during stormy weather in 1554. Recent underwater excavations of one ship, the *San Esteban*, yielded 13 tons of artifacts during two archeological field seasons.

The efforts of Spanish colonialists to protect their interests, to proselytize, and to pacify native Indians brought about the building of missions and accompanying **presidios**. On the coastal plain, Presidio Loreto was founded on the earlier site of La Salle's **palisaded** Fort Saint Louis, which is dated to the 1680s. The La Bahia mission was established near this location for coastal Indian groups. These establishments were then moved to the Victoria area in 1726 to serve inland groups, such as the Aranama and other Coahuiltecans, and were finally relocated at Goliad. Remains of the mission at Victoria were located, and preliminary archeological investigations have been carried out there. The mission and presidio at Goliad have been reconstructed and are preserved today as Goliad State Park.

Spanish ship

The Mexican influence on Texan cultures also has been investigated archeologically. Excavations in an urban Mexican-American barrio in Laredo revealed four phases of construction dating back to the 1840s. At that time houses were simple stone structures, and items such as Mexican-made ceramics and American and English wares were common household items. Spanish Colonial *majolicas* (lead-glazed ceramics), manufactured in Mexico, were uncommon.

Mexicans established Fort Lipantitlan on the lower Nueces River near San Patricio. The fort was captured by Texans in 1835, ordered to be destroyed by Mexico, and then defended from Mexican attack in 1842. The site has been located, but it has been largely destroyed by vandals. In order to protect it, the area has been designated a State Historic Site by the Texas Parks and Wildlife Department.

Following the Battle of San Jacinto, Mexico believed that parts of Texas, especially those between

Underwater excavation

the Nueces and the Rio Grande, should belong to Mexico. In April of 1846 General Zachary Taylor, marching to relieve beseiged troops led by Major Brown, skirmished with the Mexican General Arista in the Palo Alto area above Matamoros. Taylor overwhelmed the Mexicans, but Brown was killed; and Fort Brown, later established at Brownsville, was named in his honor. Archeological efforts to locate one of the battlefields in an area that has been modified significantly since the 1840s has resulted in only a minimum of artifacts that may have been associated with this event.

Fort McIntosh, another important early military site, was established in Laredo as Camp Crawford in 1849, and renamed McIntosh the following year. Archeological investigations at the site revealed both pre- and post-Civil War artifacts. Little evidence, however, was found of early structures, which may have been destroyed by repeated rebuildings at the location.

Settlement by Anglos of the Nueces-Guadalupe Plain began in the early nineteenth century. An **empresorial** grant of 1825 covering a large part of the Nueces River drainage prompted the founding of the colony of San Patricio. Gussettville, Oakville, and Rio Frio (now Tilden) were among the earliest communities settled in the area and dated to the 1850s. At Yarbrough Bend on the Frio River, ruins of at least ten homesites were excavated as part of a large Choke Canyon archeological project. Many early ranching sites exist in South Texas,

empresorial having the form of an agreement to recruit settlers and build a settlement.

Mission Espada in San Antonio

although relatively few have been documented. Research into this era of South Texas history would make an important contribution.

The introduction of the railroad stimulated change in South Texas. Victorian, Italianate, and Romanesque styles of architicture appeared within the Laredo barrio and are directly associated with the advent of the railroad there in 1881. The town called Three Rivers was founded in Live Oak County in 1913 after the railroad's arrival. In addition, oil and gas exploration gave birth to new communities and re-vitalized old towns.

The information that archeological research provides illumi-nates both prehistory and history. In spite of not being well studied for many years, prehistoric archeological sites in South Texas are begin-ning to produce a substantial body of knowlege, which is added to the rich historic record.

REFERENCES

Black, Steve
1989   South Texas Plains. In *From the Gulf to the Rio Grande: Human Adaptation in Central, South, and Lower Pecos, Texas*. Assembled by T.R. Hester and D.G. Steele. Arkansas Archeological Survey, Fayetteville, Arkansas, in press.

Campbell, T.N.
1988   *The Indians of Southern Texas and Northeastern Mexico*. Texas Archeological Research Laboratory. University of Texas Press, Austin, Texas.

Fox, Daniel
1983   *Traces of Texas History: Archeological Evidence of the Past 450 Years*. Corona Publishing Co., San Antonio, Texas.

Hall, Grant, Michael Collins, and Elton Prewitt
1987   *Cultural Resource Investigations Along Drainage Improvements, Hidalgo and Willacy Counties, Texas: 1986 Investigations*. Prewitt and Associates, Inc., Reports of Investigations No. 59. Austin, Texas.

Hall, Grant, Thomas R. Hester, and Steve Black
1986   *The Prehistoric Sites at Choke Canyon Resevoir, Southern Texas: Results of Phase II Archaeological Investigations*. Center for Archaeological Research, The University of Texas at San Antonio, Choke Canyon Series No. 10. San Antonio, Texas.

Hester, Thomas R.
1980   *Digging into South Texas Prehistory: A Guide for Amateur Archaeologists*. Corona Publishing Co., San Antonio, Texas.

1981   Tradition and Diversity Among the Prehistoric Hunters and Gatherers of Southern Texas. *Plains Anthropologist* 26(92)119-128.

Highley, Lynn
1986   *Archaeological Investigations at 41LK201, Choke Canyon Reservoir, Southern Texas*. Center for Archaeological Research, The University of Texas at San Antonio, Choke Canyon Series No.11. San Antonio, Texas.

Newcomb, W.W., Jr.
1961   *The Indians of Texas: From Prehistoric to Modern Times*. University of Texas Press, Austin, Texas.

Trans-Pecos

Cultural Time Periods

LATE PREHISTORIC (A.D. 600-1500)

The beginning of the Late Prehistoric period is marked by the introduction of the bow and arrow around A.D. 600 in the archeologically rich Lower Pecos subregion. Although the cultural remains of the Lower Pecos are sometimes considered representative of the entire Trans-Pecos, a quick look at the topography and size of the region suggests that possible differences exist in cultural traits. An essentially hunting-gathering lifestyle persisted in much of the region, while significant agricultural communities developed in pockets along the Rio Grande.

Groups of Indians began to develop horticulture and agriculture in the Trans-Pecos during the Late Prehistoric period. All along the Rio Grande from El Paso to Presidio, Indians established hamlets, villages, and small *rancherias*. Archeological evidence in the El Paso area indicates that farming technology began as early as A.D. 600 with people known as the Jornada branch of the Mollogon, a culture with origins in New Mexico.

The Hueco Bolson, located between the Franklin and Hueco mountains, proved to be a significant passage in very early times. This unique area witnessed a criss-crossing of ideas and technology from Arizona, New Mexico, and Mexico, as well as other parts of Texas. Near El Paso, Hueco Tanks, a site well known for its pictographs, has been protected as a state park for many years.

The earliest sedentary villages featured pit houses, partially below-ground-level dwellings, which were either circular or rectangular in shape. The circular structures were usually entered through an opening in the roof, while the rectangular ones featured a ramp leading to the subterranean floor.

After about A.D. 1200 pit houses disappeared and contiguous above-ground **room blocks** emerged, along with better storage facilities and ceremonial structures. Excavations at sites including Hot Wells have provided a picture of a rather complex social group utilizing nearby farming land and producing pottery types typified by El Paso **Polychrome**. Many outside influences from areas to the south and west are evident among ceramic artifacts from this time.

Around A.D. 1400 the El Paso area farmers disappeared; perhaps environmental factors played a major role in their disappearance. Semi-sedentary hunting-gathering people, known collectively as the Jumanos took their place and were the Indians encountered by the Spanish in the 1500s.

At the **confluence** of the Rio Conchos and the Rio Grande in the La Junta area, other farmers began settling around A.D. 1200. These people are known archeologically as the Bravo Valley farmers.

rancheria - a settlement composed of individual dwellings of extended families.

room block - rooms with contiguous walls.

polychrome - decorated with more than one color.

confluence - the point where two or more streams flow together.

wickiup - a rounded, brush-covered shelter.

Basket and sandals from the Lower Pecos

They lived in pit houses which featured superstructures made of adobe bricks plastered with mud. Entry was achieved through the roof, which was constructed of plastered brush.

Even though these people raised corn, beans, and squash, the uncertainty of weather demanded that their diet be supplemented by traditional hunting, gathering, and fishing. All kinds of seeds, fruits, and roots were collected. Nearby river environments provided shellfish as well as fish.

From analysis of pottery types and stone used for points and tools, archeologists have determined that trade networks were well established. The waterways provided conduits for contacting other groups living to the west and south. Many beautiful ceramic vessels originating in New Mexico and Chihuahua found their way into the region.

The vast area of the Trans-Pecos to the east of El Paso was occupied by hunter-gatherer groups who are not well known archeologically. Recent investigations, however, in the Rosillos Mountains have shown various patterns of adaptation used by the Indians of the Big Bend area. An overlapping series of hearths provides evidence of repeated use of sites in the basin. One of the most intriguing features is the circular rock alignments with entrance ways. These alignments have been interpreted as house circles, or **wickiup** rings. Around Van Horn, rock art has been documented, while sites related to the salt resources in the Guadalupe Mountains have received some study. Whether the Late Prehistoric Indians who used these varied sites were all related has not been proven archeologically, although they are thought to have been highly mobile. Some of them probably spent winters in the La Junta area and were thus in contact with the Rio Grande farmers.

In the Lower Pecos the Late Archaic lifestyle (with the important addition of the bow and arrow) continued into the first half of the Late Prehistoric period. Fortunately, suitably dry conditions in many sites have preserved not only the stone points but also the cane arrow shafts, as well as many perishable artifacts which are usually lost. Very little pottery was used, but containers did exist in the form of gourds, baskets, and some wooden items.

Toward the middle of the period certain changes appear in archeological sites and suggest that a culturally different group of people had drifted into the area. Rock art moved from the heroic-sized Pecos River Style to a more naturalistic depiction of animals and people in the Red Monochrome style. Miniature stick figures of the Red Linear style also appear. These changes occurred about the time the bison began to reappear in southwest Texas, and it is probable that the new cultural manifestations resulted from intrusive groups following the herds. Throughout the Late Prehistoric period the Indian groups continued to exploit the resources of the extensive river and canyon systems. Early historic accounts describe fishing techniques using weirs and the oxygen-depriving properties of the lechuguilla, so it is possible that these techniques were also followed in Late Prehistoric times. Upland areas, river terraces, and rock shelters were selected as camping sites, while valuable veins of chert found in the canyons served as quarries.

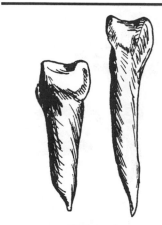

awl - a sharp-pointed bone tool.

Bone awls

HISTORIC PERIOD (A.D. 1500 - present)

The period from the early 1500s to the early 1700s was a time of initial contact between Spanish explorers and aboriginal inhabitants. Seeking gold, glory, and converts to Christianity, the Spanish provided the first written accounts of the Trans-Pecos.

The early explorer Espejo crossed the region several times on his way back and forth from Mexico to New Mexico. On one of his expeditions, he met a group of Indians near the Pecos River who called themselves Jumanos. These Indians led the Spaniards to their *rancheria* located close to Toyah Creek, where Espejo reported that dances and a feast were held in their honor. The next day, led by the Jumano guides, the Spanish party continued on through the Trans-Pecos region and finally reached the Rio Grande. The Jumanos ranged over a huge territory following the bison herds, although they were reported to have semi-permanent settlements on the Nueces River.

Another Spanish expedition traveling through the Trans-Pecos encountered a group of farming Indians at La Junta. The Patarabueye were living in pit houses averaging about 3.5 meters by 4.5 meters (11 feet by 14 feet), usually built side by side, similar to the Bravo Valley Indians of the preceding period. The Patarabueye cultivated crops such as maize, beans, watermelons, pumpkins, and tobacco. They gathered wild berries, mesquite beans, prickly pear fruit, and mushrooms to supplement their crops. Probably one of the best known sites of this culture is the Millington site, located just east of Presidio on the low terrace of the Rio Grande. This site has yielded numerous artifacts such as **awls**, *manos*, *metates*, snub-nosed scrapers, double-pointed knives, and axes.

As European countries began to compete for land in the New World, many of the Indian tribes were forced out of their territory. The tribes began to fight each other to gain new territories. The Apaches and Comanches both claimed the Trans-Pecos as their domain. They raided the agricultural villages in Northern Mexico and attacked parties passing through the Big Bend area. One of their routes became known as the

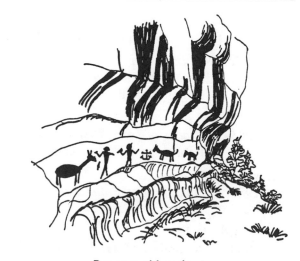

Dry cave with rock art

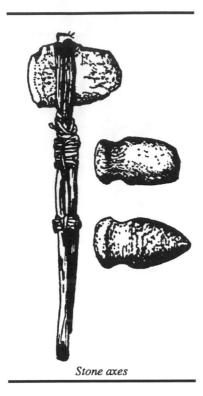

Stone axes

Comanche War Trail and extended 200 miles from the Rio Grande to the northeast.

In 1854 General Persifor Smith, commanding the Department of Texas, decided military protection for the Trans-Pecos was needed. The Comanches and Apaches were attacking mail, freight, and pioneers on the trails. On October 23, 1854, Smith commanded six companies of the U.S. Eighth Infantry under the direction of Colonel Seawell to erect a new fort, roughly midway between the Pecos River and El Paso. It was named Fort Davis in honor of Jefferson Davis. Following abandonment of this post during the Civil War, a new fort was constructed near the original site. Today Fort Davis is a historic site that is preserved by the National Park Service as an example of a typical western military fort.

Fort Leaton, a few miles from Presidio, was once thought to be a Spanish hacienda because of its appearance. Several families had owned the complex, but it was not until excavation in the 1970s that historical records of its use could be substantiated. The fort had served as an important post on the Chihuahua Trail linking Mexican and American settlements.

Cattlemen began to move in, buy land, and establish ranches, but soon the intensity of cattle grazing adversely affected the land. Many of the ranchers were forced to drive their cattle to market. Research at the Buttrill Ranch complex in the Big Bend has provided clues to some pioneer lifeways. There, three adobe structures and one feature yielded ceramic dinnerware, tin cans, and fragments of colored glass. Although more people began to homestead land and establish townships, the Trans-Pecos has remained a challenge for the men and women who attempted to settle it.

REFERENCES

Campbell, T.N.
   1970   *Archeological Survey of the Big Bend National Park, 1966-1967.* Two Parts. Report submitted to the National Park Service by the University of Texas at Austin, Austin, Texas.

Fox, Daniel
   1983   *Traces of Texas History: Archeological Evidence of the Past 450 Years.* Corona Publishing Co., San Antonio, Texas.

Kelley, J. Charles
   1985   *Jumanos and Patarabueye, Relations at La Junta De Los Rios.* University of Michigan, Ann Arbor, Michigan.

Lehmer, Donald J.
   1960   A Review of Trans-Pecos Texas Archeology. *Bulletin of the Texas Archeological Society* 29:109-144.

Mallouf, Robert J.
1981   Observations Concerning Environmental and Cultural Interactions During the Terminal Pleistocene and Early Holocene in the Big Bend of Texas and Adjoining Regions. *Bulletin of the Texas Archeological Society* 52:121-146.

Mallouf, Robert J., and Virginia A. Wulfkuhle
1989   An Archeological Reconnaissance in the Rosillos Mountains, Brewster County, Texas. *The Journal of Big Bend Studies*, Vol. 1. Sul Ross State University, Alpine, Texas.

Museum of the Big Bend
1978   *Indian Life in the Texas Big Bend.* Sul Ross State University, Alpine, Texas.

Shafer, Harry J.
1986   *Ancient Texans: Rock Art and Lifeways Along the Lower Pecos.* Texas Monthly Press, Austin, Texas.

Turpin, Solveig A.
1982   *Seminole Canyon: The Art and Archeology, Val Verde County, Texas.* Texas Archeological Survey, Research Report No. 83. Austin, Texas.

Tyler, Ronnie C.
1975   *The Big Bend: A History of the Last Texas Frontier.* National Park Service, U.S. Department of the Interior, Washington, D.C.

Utley, Robert
1985   *If These Walls Could Speak: Historic Forts of Texas.* University of Texas Press, Austin, Texas.

Whalen, Michael E.
1977   *Settlement Patterns of the Eastern Hueco Bolson.* Anthropological Paper Number 4, Centennial Museum, University of Texas at El Paso, El Paso, Texas.

Williams-Dean, Glenna
1978   *Ethnobotony and Cultural Ecology of Prehistoric Man in Southwest Texas.* Ph.D. dissertation. Texas A&M University, College Station, Texas.

Wulfkuhle, Virginia
1986   *The Buttrill Ranch Complex, Brewster County, Texas: Evidence of Early Ranching in the Big Bend.* Texas Historical Commission, Austin, Texas.

Section III
ACTIVITIES

Photo by Elton Prewitt

INDEX OF ACTIVITIES

★★Those activities recommended for 10 day unit.

INTRODUCTION

This activities section will provide classroom lessons to parallel the methodology of archeologists. Lessons for ten class periods (45-60 min.) have been selected and noted to form a unit, but many other activities may be used to enrich or supplement the basic concepts. Try to use at least one activity from each sub-section so that you will carry out the process of an archeological investigation from Survey through Preservation.

Appropriate grade levels and subjects are designated for each activity. A preparation section supplies background information on archeology as well as materials and references needed. Objectives and procedures are outlined in a step-by-step fashion to facilitate each lesson.

Specialized vocabulary is set in bold type and these words are listed in each lesson and are defined in the Glossary. Numerous teacher resources are found in the Appendix, including Juvenile Fiction, Magazines, Articles, Published Teaching Units, Replica Artifacts, Audio Visuals, and Local Societies. Some technical information on archeology from the Texas Historical Commission is also included.

ACTIVITIES SELECTED TO FORM A 10-DAY UNIT

Activity: Backyard Archeology

Levels: Grades 3-8

Subjects: Language Arts, Science, Social Studies, Fine Arts

Objectives: During this activity students will: (1) describe physical **features** of a landscape, (2) show awareness of the man-made environment, and (3) arrange ideas and information.

PREPARATION:

Background: One of the first things archeologists do at a **site** is a visual **survey**. They make note of and map all standing structures and above-ground **artifacts.** From this information they can begin to get an idea of the use or function of the site even before excavation.

Materials: Activity sheet with backyards showing some above-ground artifacts (swing set, garden, fountain, etc.)

Procedure: (1)   Have students study the drawings. Who might live there?
                (2)   How did the students guess who the occupants might be? Define features and site in terms of the backyard.
                (3)   Have each student identify and list at least three artifacts.
                (4)   Ask students to relate what each artifact tells about the people who used the site.
                (5)   Have them explain their conclusions.

Vocabulary: artifact
                  feature
                  site
                  survey

Name ——————————————————————————— Date ——————

BACKYARD ARCHEOLOGY

Look at the drawings of two backyards. What conclusions can you draw about the people who used these sites?

Features	Interpretation/meaning

1.

2.

3.

Features	Interpretation/meaning

1.

2.

3.

Vocabulary: artifact
                feature
                site
                survey

Activity: Survey the School Grounds

Levels: Grades 3-8

Subjects: Fine Arts, Mathematics, Social Studies, Science

Objectives: While recording placement of structures and objects to predict **functional** use of an area, students will use: (1) their awareness of the natural and man-made environment, (2) measurement concepts and skills, (3) mapping skills: directions, scale and compass rose, and (4) logical inferences to form generalized statements.

PREPARATION:

Background: Archeologists predict the function of a site by recording **features** and **artifacts** to see if patterns develop.

Materials: Meter tapes
                Graph paper,
                Sack for collection of material (one per group).

References: Hester (1980)
                Hester, Heizer, and Graham (1975)

Procedures: (1) Divide the students into 4 to 6 groups.
                (2) Send each group to a specific location* (a-f) where they will record the physical **features** by description and collect **artifacts** (trash).
                (3) When they return to the classroom, have each group present their artifactual collection and description (labeled only with the letter designations a-f for purpose of secrecy) to the class so that class members may guess the location and function of each area (a-f).

                * Possible site locations:
                a) playground   d) art class
                b) athletic field   e) nurse's office
                c) cafeteria   f) classroom at different levels

Vocabulary: artifact
                feature
                function

Survey ★

Activity:	How Sites Are Formed
Levels:	Grades 3-8
Subjects:	Language Arts, Science, Social Studies, Fine Arts
Objectives:	In describing clues left behind, the student will: (1) inform by using description, (2) predict outcome, and (3) identify **customs**.

PREPARATION:

Background: An archeological **site** is the place where evidence of human activity can be found. This evidence is recognized as patterns (**features**) and objects (**artifacts**) left behind. Students understand the connection between human activity and archeological sites when they can relate the process to their world. Using school or family activities and predicting clues which would remain teaches the concept of site formation.

Materials: Paper for list

References: Fagan (1978)
Hole and Heizer (1965)

Procedure:
(1) Divide students into groups to consider one of the following "sites":
   a. a dance in the school gym
   b. a family picnic in the park
   c. a lost football game
   d. a factory after an explosion
   e. a fire in an apartment building
   f. a strong campaign speech
(2) On a sheet of paper, have students write down all the different clues which might remain.
(3) Have the students summarize things you can tell by **physical remains** and things you can not (emotions, thoughts). Similar evidence remains in archeological sites, therefore, the picture is often incomplete.

Vocabulary: artifact
custom
feature
physical remains
site

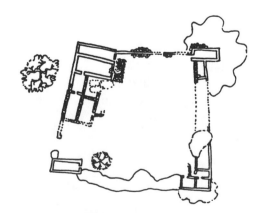

Activity: Site Types

Levels: Grades 3-8

Subjects: Language Arts, Social Studies, Science

Objectives: The students will (1) learn about types of **sites** which are found by archeologists, (2) show awareness of natural and man-made environments, and (3) predict what types of sites our current living patterns will leave.

PREPARATION:

Background: People throughout the time have had to satisfy their basic needs for shelter, food, clothing, protection, and explanation of the supernatural. When archeologists go in the field, they look for patterns which might reveal these activities to them. These basic site types are **occupation** (village), brief occupation (campsite), place of worship, location for burial, trash disposal (**midden**), food preparation, and tool making. We have similar needs today. Can you identify what evidence we would leave behind?

Materials: Activity Sheet

References: Hester (1980)
               Vander-Meulen (1983)
               Zappler and Simons (1984)

Procedure: (1) Discuss basic needs with students and list these on the board.
               (2) Have the students think about categories for these needs and develop a chart that shows current evidence of satisfying our needs. Add the clues that may be found archeologically to show how early people also satisfied these basic needs.

Vocabulary: midden
               occupation
               site

Teacher Key: Basic Human Needs: food, clothing, shelter, protection, leisure, and explanation of the supernatural (religion). Please refer to the drawings on the next page.

Some Native American activities and items which satisfy basic human needs

Activities

Activity: Predictions: Reading Between the Lines

Levels: Grades 6-8

Subjects: Language Arts, Social Studies, Science

Objectives: The student will (1) obtain data from varied sources, and (2) will use written records to predict archeological remains.

PREPARATION:

Background: Archeologists read journals and history books when considering an area for investigation. Clues to sites are often found as the authors describe places they lived and routes they traveled. Archeologists locate and investigate sites to verify the written record and expand ideas about how the people lived. Sites which have been described in written accounts include ancient sites in literature (Troy), fortifications of empires (Roman in England), colonization (Jamestown, Columbus in West Indies), historic Indians (Apache), and early settlements (Strawberry Banks, NH).

Materials: References with accounts of early expeditions and surveys of the study area

References: **Zappler and Simons (1984)**
               Newcomb (1961)

Procedures: Read aloud to students from a journal or diary about an early expedition to a selected area. As you read, have the students list or draw **artifacts** and **features** they would expect to find at a site. Compare their predictions with recorded sites. Emphasize types of materials that do remain and the information that can be gained from those **assemblages.**

Vocabulary: artifacts
               assemblage
               feature

Name _____ Date _____

PREDICTIONS

Read an account of an early expedition to your area. As the descriptions of the land, structures, inhabitants, and customs are related, list (or draw) features and artifacts that you would expect to find, based on the historic accounts.

<table>
<tr><td>

</td><td></td></tr>
<tr><td>

</td><td></td></tr>
</table>

Vocabulary: artifacts
                  features

Activity: Ecological Survey

Levels: Grades 3-8

Subjects: Language Arts, Social Studies, Science

Objectives: The student will (1) observe the types of plant and animal communities in a specific
                 area, (2) record the information requested for a site report, and (3) identify which natural
                 features and resources would be helpful to early inhabitants.

PREPARATION:

Background: Early people depended much more directly on the land for their survival and well being.
             It is important that archeologists look at the land and ask questions about the potential of
             the environment.

Materials: Activity Sheet

References: McHargue and Roberts (1977)

Procedures: (1) Have the students imagine an area familiar to the class or visit a nearby natural
                      reserve (park, undeveloped land, etc.).
                 (2) Divide the students into teams of 5 to 6 students to work together on a set of ques-
                      tions adapted from standard site forms, as described below.

                      A. Site description—fully describe the nature of the site and its setting.
                      B. Vegetation—fully describe the nature of the site and its setting.
                      C. Water—note the direction, distance and nature of the nearest fresh water
                          supply.
                      D. Soil—describe the type of soil found.
                      E. Erosion and disturbance—describe any erosion visible.
                      F. Cultivation—if the land is being farmed, list the crops and seasons the
                          land is used.

                 (3) Review the information which the students recorded and direct them to take the next
                      step and relate how early inhabitants might have used the land. How would this
                      type of thinking help archeologists in the field?

Vocabulary: ecology

Name _____ Date _____

ECOLOGICAL SURVEY

These questions are found on standard site forms used to report archeological sites. Practice your skills of observation and deduction by supplying the following data:

A. Site description

B. Vegetation

C. Water Source

D. Soil Type

E. Erosion

F. Cultivation

What were the advantages of this site to early inhabitants?

Vocabulary: ecology

Activity: Visible Clues

Levels: Grades 3-8

Subjects: Language Arts, Science

Objectives: The students will be able to: (1) classify information by likeness and differences, (2) describe changes in environment, (3) describe physical features, and (4) name economic resources.

PREPARATION:

Background: Archeologists look for vegetation clues to help them locate sites. There are some predictors which suggest areas to investigate. These clues include:

a)   crops come up earlier and stay greener where there are ancient pits or trenches filled with soil, hence organically rich soil.

b)   crops come up later and fade earlier when they grow above ancient walls (shallow soil).

c)   plants grow shorter over buried road surfaces or ancient walls (little soil).

d)   faint ground markings visible only from the air indicate places where buildings once stood; therefore, aerial photography should be used to survey an area.

Materials: Activity sheet which illustrates various situations listed below.

References: Cork and Reid (1984)
              Hole and Heizer (1965)
              Sylvester (1982)

Procedures: Show students the sketches and ask them to predict what remains might be under the ground.

Extension: In some areas there are local sayings about potential sites, for example, Spanish dagger plant grows on Indian mounds. Have students collect these sayings and see if there could be some truth to them.

Name _____ Date _____

VISIBLE CLUES

Looking at the sketches of vegetation on specific sites, what type of feature would you expect to find underground?
(adapted from Cork and Reid)

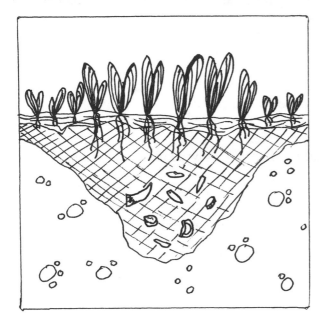

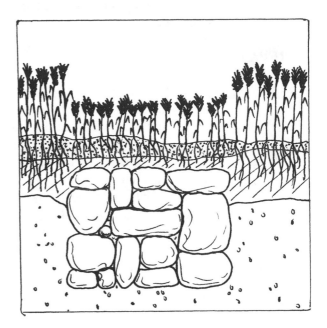

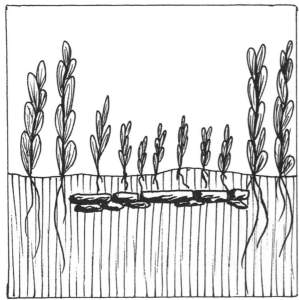

Activity: Locate a Site

Levels: Grade 3-8

Subjects: Language Arts, Fine Arts, Social Studies, Science

Objectives: The student will: (1) use graphic sources for information, (2) predict outcomes, (3) show awareness of natural and man-made environments, (4) describe **physical features**, and (5) identify multiple causes of events.

PREPARATION:

Background: Ancient people selected areas in which to settle for much the same reasons we do today. These reasons include: 1) near water source, 2) close to fertile soil, 3) easily defensible, and 4) on a trade route.

Materials :   **Topographic map** of study area; political map of study area. Catalogs with maps:

U.S. Geological Survey
Box 25425, Federal Center
Denver, CO 80225
(303) 236-7476
(topo maps)

Geographic Computer Search
EROS Data Center
Sioux Fall, S.D. 57198
(satellite photos)

References: **Cork and Reid (1984)**
Hole and Heizer (1965)
Vander-Meulen (1983)
Nichols (1988)

Procedures: (1) Have students view the **topographic** map and predict where at least three sites or settlements might be located.
(2) Compare predictions with a political map of the same area to see if settlements (towns) are where they predicted.

Extension: In many cases, when a town was destroyed by a disaster, people settled at the same site later. Why?

Vocabulary: physical feature
topographic map

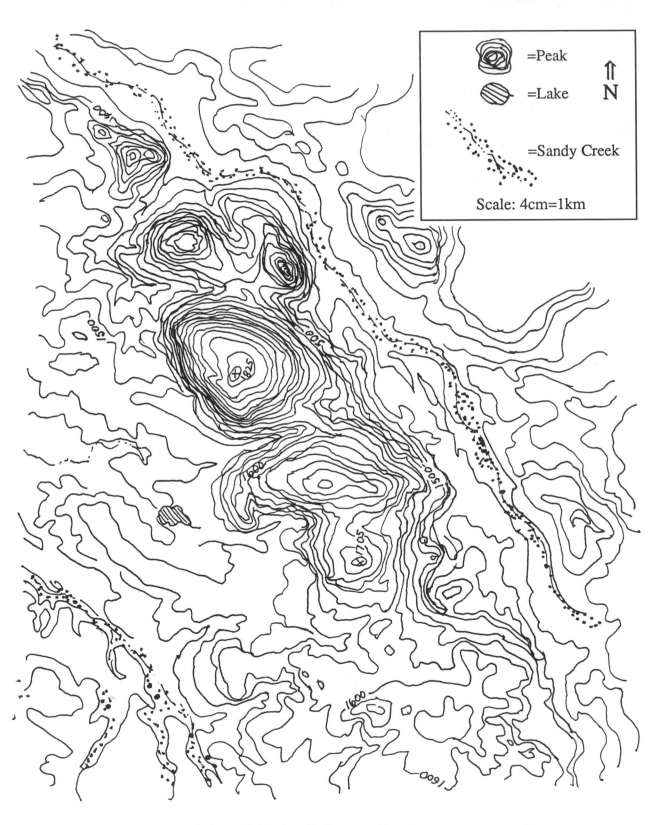

Sketch of a typical topographic map

Activities

Activity: Methods of Survey

Levels: Grades 6-12

Subjects: Language Arts, Social Studies, Science

Objectives: The student will: (1) learn technical methods of **survey**, (2) use a variety of sources for research, and (3) gain experience in communicating data.

PREPARATION:

Background: Science has aided archeologists in discovering sites and pinpointing **features** such as houses. Numerous methods of survey, while expensive, can be utilized.

References: Hemion (1983)
             Hester, Heizer, and Graham (1975)

Procedures: Have students research the following special techniques of survey and explain the procedures to the class. Have them emphasize <u>how</u> the method helps archeologists locate a site. Visual aids would enrich the presentation. Topics to consider:
1. aerial photography
2. magnetometry
3. resistivity
4. thermography
5. SLAR
6. LANDSAT
7. Lerici periscope

Vocabulary: feature
                survey

Survey ★

Activity: Recording a Survey

Levels: Grades 6-12

Subjects: Language Arts, Mathematics, Social Studies, Science

Objectives: The students will (1) use description to inform, (2) use the metric system for measurement, (3) map and record locations of objects, (4) use directions, compass, scale and grid, and (5) demonstrate respect for private property.

PREPARATION:

Background: All sites should be reported to the central state agency which compiles information for research purposes. This agency has a form which helps standardize the information. Students are often aware of sites which have not been recorded. To locate and record a site would be a model lesson in preservation.

Materials: Archeological Site Data Form
Source for Form:
      Texas Archeological Research Laboratory
      10100 Burnet Road, Austin, Texas 78758.
Topographic map of area
Compass
Metric tape measures

References: Hester (1980)
Hemion (1983)

Procedures: (1) Select a site that the class may visit easily. This could be an old homestead, a scatter of Indian artifacts or military items, etc.

(2) Contact the land owner for permission to go on the land. Assure the land owner that your intention is reporting for research only and that no artifacts will be removed.

(3) Locate a person with experience in recording sites to assist in the field work involved. The following steps should be followed:

    a) review the forms so that students will be familiar with the information needed

    b) assemble materials and equipment needed to record accurately the information

    c) arrange a field trip to the site according to school policy

    d) announce rules regarding "collecting", i.e. map and photograph artifacts but leave them in place

    e) document the site on the form

    f) mail the form and documentary evidence to the state agency (Texas Archeological Research Laboratory)

Activity: Locations on a Grid

Levels: Grades 3-8

Subjects: Mathematics, Science, Social Studies, Language Arts

Objectives: The students will (1) learn to use **grid coordinates** to locate objects and (2) understand
               the importance of mapping artifacts so that patterns will be recorded.

PREPARATION:

Background: One of the most important aspects of excavating a site is to record all patterns that
             appear. Since the **context** of the site is destroyed when excavation occurs, every detail
             must be accurately noted. This activity will introduce students to the concept of a grid.

Materials: Activity Sheet

Procedures: (1) Discuss maps and uses of maps in general terms of location.
               (2) Give students the Activity Sheet and work the first number with them. Encourage
                   them to complete the exercise.
               (3) Summarize the lesson by talking about the importance of mapping in recording
                   archeological sites.

Vocabulary: context
               coordinates
               grid

Teacher Key for Activity Sheet:
               1. Small pot 1D, 2D
               2. The sun 4A
               3. The bow 3C, 3D, 4C
               4. A projectile point 3A
               5. A basket 2B
               6. Water 1A, 1B

ACTIVITY SHEET

Name ——————————————————— Date ———————————————

LOCATION ON A GRID

A grid is superimposed over a site before excavation units are started. This grid-map allows archeologists to record the exact location of the units.

For practice, see if you can name the grid square(s) or units where the Indian designs are located.
1. small pot _____ _____
2. the sun _____
3. the bow _____ _____ _____
4. a projectile point _____
5. a basket _____ _____
6. water _____

Activity: Cultural Puzzle

Levels: Grades 5-8

Subjects: Science, Social Studies, Mathematics, Language Arts

Objectives: The students will (1) classify materials according to **function**, (2) predict a **chronological** sequence for materials, and (3) present conclusions to the class.

PREPARATION:

Background: For each **cultural** time period (Paleoindian, Archaic, Late Prehistoric, Historic) there can be a generalized set of artifacts (see following pages for suggestions). The assumption is that each **assemblage** represented was removed from a defined **occupation** and is ready for analysis.

Prepare an **assemblage** (pictures and artifacts in a shoe box OR have artifacts to bury in **units**) for each cultural time period. Label these with colors. These will be analyzed by the students in groups.

Materials: Sheet with **assemblage** for analysis OR as many **unprovenienced artifacts** as possible
Record sheet

References: Lipetzky (1982)
Hemion (1983)
Hester (1980)

Procedures: (1) Divide the students into "crews" of 3 to 4. Give each crew a box or assign them a unit.
(2) Have students work together to excavate or review the assemblage of artifacts. Precision depends on the age of the students and the purpose of the exercise. Measurement and mapping may be required if the unit is in the ground or if the artifacts are laid out as a unit.
(3) As artifacts are available have the students record the materials on the chart as to function—shelter, food, etc.

Vocabulary: artifacts   function
assemblage   occupation
chronological   (un) provenience
culture   unit

Teacher Key: Cultural Time-Line for Texas (Generalized)
Yellow— Paleoindian 10,000 B.C.-6,000 B.C.
Blue—   Archaic 6,000 B.C.-A.D. 500
Red—   Late Prehistoric A.D. 500-1500
Green—   Historic (Mission) A.D. 1500-1800

Name _____ Date _____

Cultural Puzzle Chart

| Culture Time Period ? | Food Clothing | Shelter: Location Style | Technology | | Status: Government Religion Military | Aesthetics: Art Jewelry Games Ritual |
			Tools Weapons	Pottery		
Red						
Yellow						
Green						
Blue						

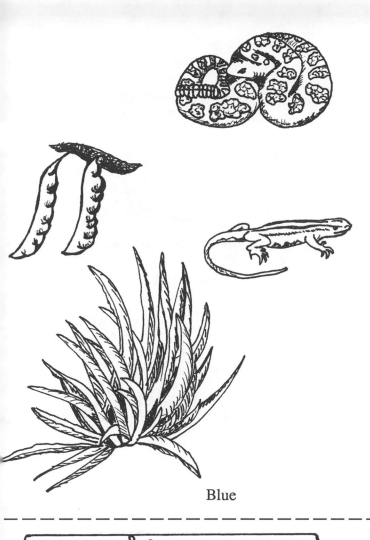

Blue

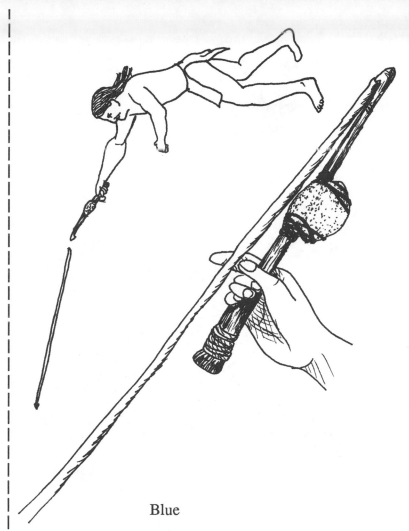

Blue

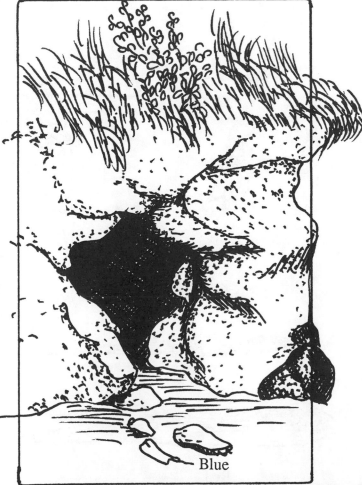

Blue

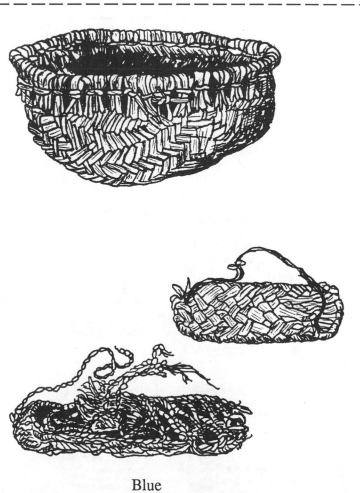

Blue

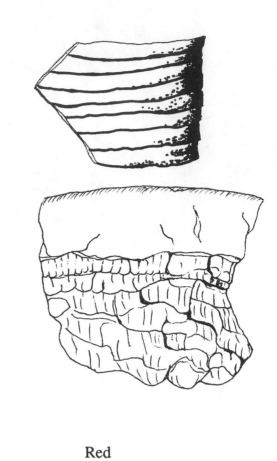

Red

Red

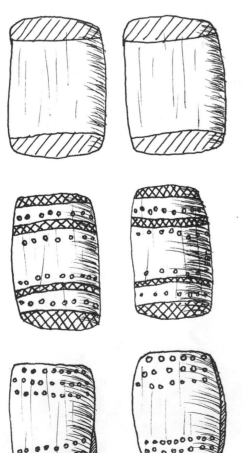

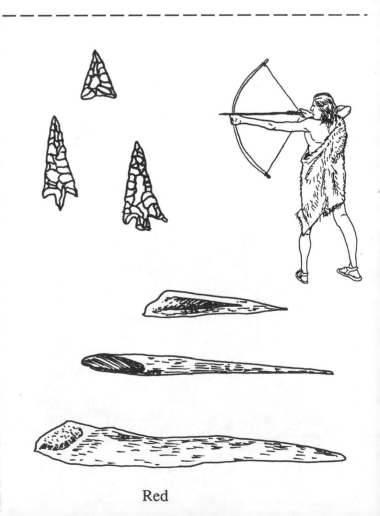

Red

Red

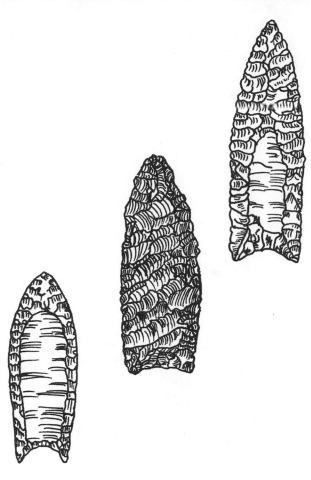

Yellow

Yellow

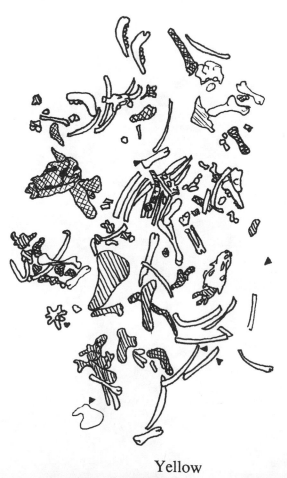

Yellow

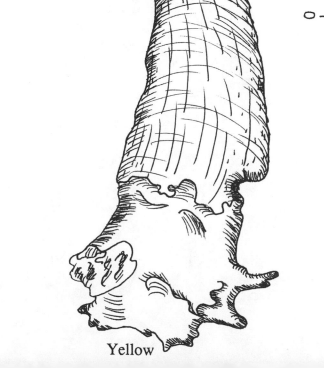

Yellow

Green

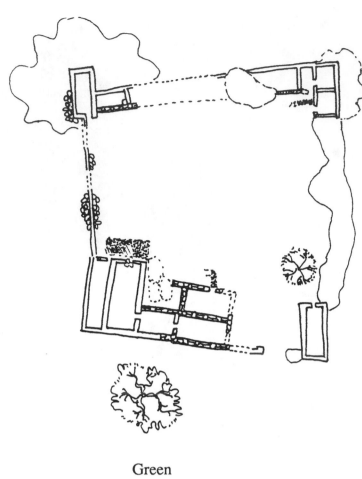

Green

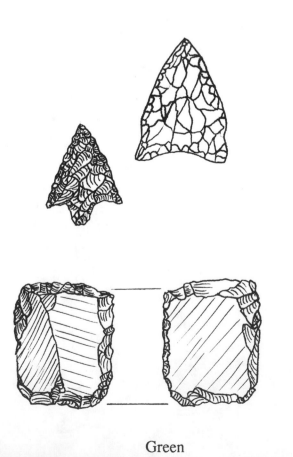

Green

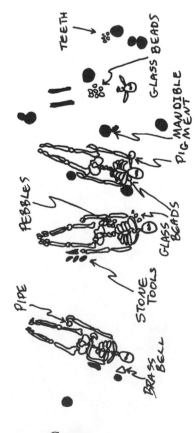

Green

Activity: Site Profile

Levels: Grades 6-8

Subjects: Language Arts, Social Studies, Science

Objectives: The students will (1) use graphic sources for information, (2) use classification skills in organizing and sequencing data, (3) describe some ways one's community has changed over time, and (4) use mapping skills to relate information.

PREPARATION:

Background: When a **unit** is excavated one wall is usually left in place so that it can be drawn in profile. This drawing (**profile**) shows the layers (**strata**) as they have been exposed in excavation.

Materials: Activity Sheet

References: Cork and Reid (1984)
             Vander-Meulen (1983)
             Zappler and Simons (1984)

Procedures: (1) Explain the definition and importance of the profile which shows the strata as they might be found in an area.
                 (2) The strata are labelled with the surface at the top, in descending order: surface / mission / Late Prehistoric / Archaic / Paleoindian.
                 (3) Ask students to draw in or label each artifact listed into the appropriate strata.

Extension: Have students place a date or time period for each stratum.

Vocabulary: profile, strata, unit

Teacher Key: 1) Mission— gun flint   2) Late Prehistoric—woven mat
                            chicken bone   clam shells
                            Spanish pottery   rock art
                            metal cross   cemetery
                            cemetery   bison bones
                            glass beads   small arrow point
                                                                           deer bones
                                                                           poorly fired pottery
                 3) Archaic— clam shells
                            bison bones
                            deer bones   4) Paleoindian— bison bones
                            dart point   spear point
                            fire hearth

Name _____ Date _____

SITE PROFILE

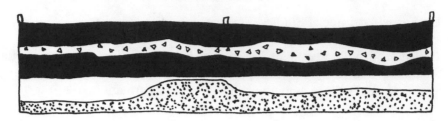

Below is a diagram of strata found at a site. Using the list of artifacts, draw or label the location of each object listed.

woven mat	rock art	dart point
gun flint	cemetery	fire hearth
chicken bone	bison bones	spear point
Clovis point	small arrow point	
clam shells	glass beads	
Spanish pottery	deer bones	
metal cross	poorly fired pottery	

Surface

Mission (1)

Late Prehistoric (2)

Archaic (3)

Paleoindian (4)

<u>Extension</u>: Identify the approximate time period for each stratum.

Activity: Surface Mapping

Levels: Grades 3-8

Subjects: Mathematics, Social Studies, Science

Objectives: The student will (1) use the metric system for measuring, (2) measure and map the location of objects, and (3) predict outcome.

PREPARATION:

Background: Since site deposits are destroyed during **excavation**, care must be taken to record every detail beginning with the initial **survey**. The first step at the site is to map the surface. This is accomplished most easily with a **grid** superimposed over the site.

Materials: graph paper (optional)
metric tapes
string

References: Hemion (1983)
Hester (1980)
Hester, Heizer, and Graham (1975)

Procedures: (1) Have the students consider the classroom a site. Lay out a grid in the room with intersecting string at regular intervals (1 or 2 meters).
(2) Ask the students to map classroom furniture. The teacher may choose to lead this activity with a map on the overhead projector. For independent practice, have each student map his/her bedroom in the same fashion.

Extension: Have students predict ten objects which would last 1,000 years. For example, what would archeologists find in A.D. 3,000 to tell them about the students in the class (classroom) or individual (bedroom) of today.

Vocabulary: excavation
grid
survey

Excavation ★

Activity: Trash Can Dig

Levels: Grades 3-8

Subjects: Social Studies, Science

Objectives: The students will (1) demonstrate their understanding of **stratigraphy**, (2) interpret materials found in wastebaskets, and (3) categorize these materials according to function.

PREPARATION:

Background: People who do not have a garbage collection system throw their trash in heaps and pits. Garbage dumps (**middens**) are a rich source of information for archeologists. In most deposits the materials on the top are the youngest (most recent). Those on the bottom are the oldest. This layering is known as stratigraphy and is called the law of superposition.

Materials: One or more wastebaskets
             Activity Sheet

Procedures: (1) Collect wastebaskets which have been prepared for one week with only paper (avoid food stuff) from predetermined locations.
             (2) Have student "excavate" (or observe you in the process of excavating) a waste basket.
             (3) Ask these questions:
                 What items were thrown in first? This is the earliest strata.
                 What can you tell about the activities that took place in the room?
                 Where was the wastebasket kept?
                 What do these remains tell us about how the people lived?

Vocabulary: midden
             stratigraphy

Extension: A dirty clothes hamper is an additional analogy showing stratification. Presumably those clothes worn most recently will be on top.

Name _____ Date _____

TRASH CAN DIG

People throw trash away when it is no longer of use to them. Areas where trash builds up are called **middens**. These areas are a rich source of information for archeologists. Can you guess why?

In our homes and classrooms we put trash in wastebaskets and trash cans. To look at a sample of what archeologists find in midden areas, sort through the contents of a wastebasket. As you "excavate" the wastebasket, keep a record of the layers (**strata**) by dividing it into thirds. Complete the diagram below as you sort.

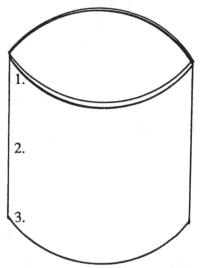

1. Which layer (strata) had the oldest material?

2. What activities can be identified from each strata?

(1)

(2)

(3)

3. What can you tell about the people who used this wastebasket?

Excavation ★ ▬▬▬▬▬▬▬▬▬▬▬▬▬▬▬▬▬▬▬▬▬▬

Activity: Recording Artifacts

Levels: Grades 3-8

Subjects: Language Arts, Mathematics, Social Studies, Science

Objectives: The student will (1) use the metric system to measure, (2) measure and record location
                of objects, (3) practice mapping using direction, compass, scale, and grid, and (4) make
                inferences based on data.

PREPARATION:

Background: The meter square is the basic recording unit in an **excavation**. It is good preparation or
             simulation for students to record accurately objects or **artifacts** as they might appear in
             an excavation.

Materials: Objects or artifacts to map (6 to 8 per unit)
             One meter tape per unit
             Graph paper or form on which to record information

References: Hemion (1983)
             Hester (1980)

Procedures: (1) Divide students into teams of 3 to 4 people to record artifacts found in a simulated
                    unit.
                (2) Lay out a set of artifacts (by theme or randomly) on a table or desk top for each
                    student team.
                (3) Have students assist each other in plotting the artifacts on the **grid** or form. (Students
                    may each have a paper or may work as a team).
                (4) Ask students if there is a pattern or theme to the arrangement of the artifacts. What
                    conclusions or inferences could they make based on the artifacts recorded?

Vocabulary: artifact
                excavation
                grid

Name _____ Date _____

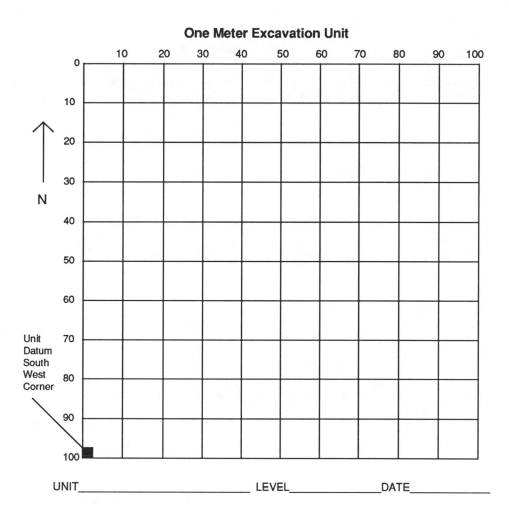

One Meter Excavation Unit

UNIT_____ LEVEL_____ DATE_____

Key	Key Symbols to Scale	Artifact #	Depth at Bottom of Artifact	#	Depth at Bottom of Artifact
○	Pottery				
△	Stone				
▭	Metal				
✕	Glass				
⟍	Bone				

Excavation ★ ▬▬▬▬▬▬▬▬▬▬▬▬▬▬▬▬

Activity: Excavation Techniques

Levels: Grades 3-8

Subjects: Language Arts, Social Studies, Science, Mathmatics

Objectives: The student will (1) observe excavation techniques, (2) learn the rationale for those
               techniques, (3) form generalized statements, and (4) give reasons to persuade.

PREPARATION:

Background: Specific techniques are used to insure preservation of materials and accuracy when
            excavating a site.

Materials : A film or slides (see audio visuals list in Appendix) on techniques to create an interest in
            the details
            Worksheet or oral discussion of questions posed below

References: Hackwell (1986)
            Hemion (1983)
            Hester (1980)
            Zappler and Simons (1984)

Procedures: Pose the following questions about **excavation** techniques to help students understand
               the demands of archeology.

               1. When an **archeologist** finds an **artifact**, he uses a very fine tool such as a brush or
                  bamboo pick. Why?

               2. As soil is removed from an excavation unit, it is put into a bucket then sifted through
                  screen. What is the purpose of this procedure?

               3. When an artifact is found, it is measured and photographed *in situ*, exactly where it
                  was found. Why is this important?

Vocabulary: archeologist
               artifact
               excavation
               in situ

Activity: Uncovering a Feature

Levels: Grades 3-8

Subjects: Science, Social Studies, Language Arts

Objectives: The student will (1) observe the **excavation** of a **feature**, (2) predict what pattern will emerge, and (3) understand the non-portable status of a feature.

PREPARATION:

Background: Features are cultural remains more complex than a single **artifact.** Examples of features include fire **hearths**, storage pits, cooking pits, and burials. The **assemblage** of materials must be considered together for analysis and interpretation.

Materials: 3 to 6 slides of the same feature as it is being uncovered.

References: Hester (1980)

Procedures: (1) Define and discuss a feature. Give examples and relate the importance of a feature being considered with special treatment in excavation, recording, and analysis.

(2) Show slides of the uncovering of a feature at different stages. Have students predict what is buried as the details are revealed.

(3) Have students sketch the feature at the last stage. Discuss what is left to identify archeologically. Also discuss what might have been there which does not remain due to lack of preservation.

Extension: Have students reconstruct a scene of the activity that produced the feature.

Vocabulary: assemblage
artifact
excavation
feature
hearth

Analysis ★★

Activity: Artifact Identification

Levels: Grades 3-8

Subjects: Social Studies, Science, Language Arts

Objectives: The students will (1) recognize **artifacts** as human-made objects, (2) categorize artifacts according to **function** (use), and (3) understand the ambivalence of some objects when they are out of **context**.

PREPARATION:

Background: Isolated finds or artifacts removed from a **site** are sometimes difficult to identify, lose their meaning without the association of context, and can be interpreted in a variety of ways.

Materials: Objects brought to class by students

References: Weitzman (1975)

Procedure:

(1) Ask students to bring to class objects they would classify as artifacts. These may be historic or prehistoric. (Be prepared with materials to supplement the collection in case some forget.)

(2) As a class or in small groups, have students identify the objects and their use. Could they have been used for more than one purpose? What additional information could help define the function of each one?

(3) When artifacts are found *in situ* in an excavation they often have other materials with them which can help define their use. For example, a stone knife might be found with bones that have butchering marks on them. This artifact provides more information in **association** that it would if it were isolated.

Vocabulary: artifact
association
context
function
in situ

Key:
1. Rammer
2. Sheep's fork
3. Riffler
4. Round iron
5. Fish gripper
6. Folding pick
7. Diamond mortar
8. Rail fork
9. Wire potato scoop
10. Gaiter

Name: _____   Date: _____

Label these early tools and utensils and explain their use (function).

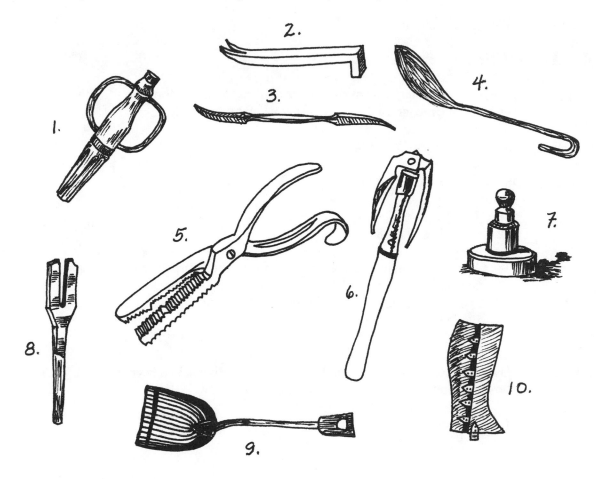

Activity: Arrow Dynamics

Levels: Grades 3-8

Subjects: Science, Social Studies

PREPARATION:

Background: Indian **spears, darts,** and **arrows** were constructed to fly "on target." This exercise will help students recognize the purpose and value of the feathers.

Materials: Straws and paper (feathers).

References: Finney and Kindle (1985)
             Hester (1980)
             Pine (1957)
             Turner and Hester (1985)

Procedures: (1) Give each student a straw. Have them throw it across the room. What happens?
             (2) Have each student cut several "fins" out of paper and insert the fins into slits in the straw.
             (3) Have the students throw the arrows again. How do the flights compare?

Extension: Have the students research aerodynamics and list five new facts they learn. Then allow the students to make an even better flying straw.

Vocabulary: arrow
             dart
             spear

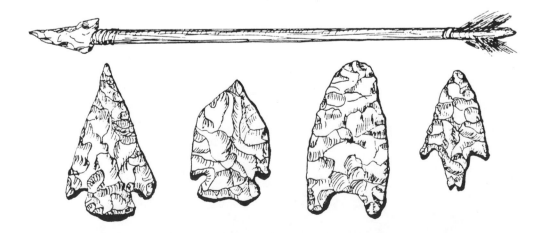

Activity: Pottery Reconstruction

Levels: Grades 3-8

Subjects: Fine Arts, Social Studies, Science, Mathematics

Objectives: The students will (1) reconstruct a broken **vessel**, (2) experience properties and relation-
                 ships of geometric shapes, (3) gain data through the senses, (4) express themselves
                 through art materials, (5) give examples of specialization, and (6) understand ways of
                 satisfying basic needs.

PREPARATION:

Background: Since **pottery** is a common artifact found on sites, archeologists often spend time in the lab
                 reconstructing vessels. Some of the information which a vessel might yield would be
                 function, origin of clay, trade patterns (if foreign), ownership based on design, or date
                 according to comparison to known pottery sequences.

Materials: Several broken vessels or flower pots, packaged with one or more piece missing
                 Glue
                 Box or a secure base to hold reconstructed pieces
                 Paper to protect work surface

References: Baylor (1972)
                 Glubok (1964)
                 Hemion (1983)
                 Hester (1980)
                 Nichols (1988)

Procedures: (1) Discuss the importance and uses of **pottery** from prehistoric to historic times,
                      concentrating on a particular culture for emphasis. Show illustrations of different
                      kinds of pottery. Relate how **pottery** helps archeologists determine spatial function,
                      for example cooking or eating area, and chronology based on comparison with
                      pottery of a known age.
                 (2) Divide students into work groups, ideally 3 or 4 students per **vessel**. Distribute
                      package of pot **sherds**. Have students reconstruct the vessel.
                 (3) After the vessel is "complete", have each group describe it according to **attributes**
                      and function, if possible.

Alternate: Draw vessels on small puzzles and have the students work the puzzle. Suggest that
                 students draw their own puzzle over a blank puzzle format.

Vocabulary: attribute
                 function
                 pottery
                 sherd
                 vessel

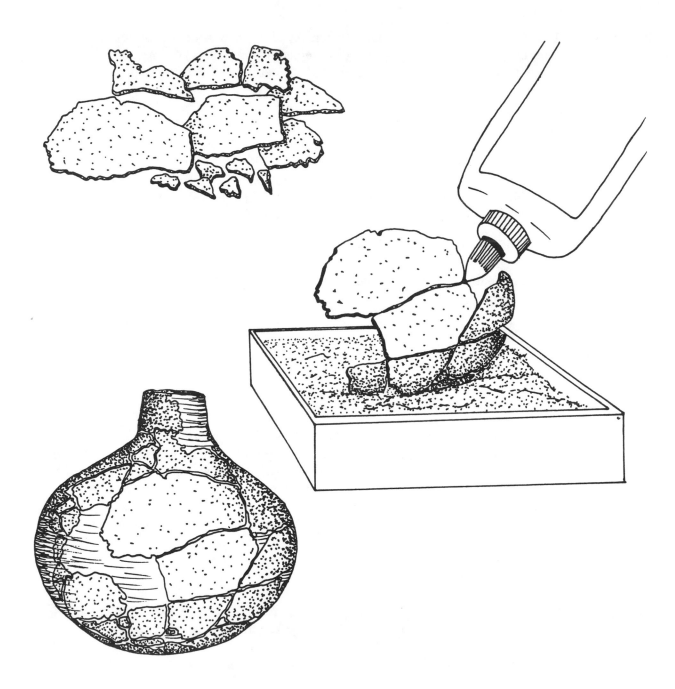

Reconstructing a vessel

Activities: Making Stone Tools

Levels: Grades 3-8

Subject: Science, Social Studies

Objectives: Students will (1) observe the process of stone tool making, (2) predict how these tools might have been used, and (3) understand how these tools change over time.

PREPARATION:

Background: Stone tools represent a major type of **artifact** found at many **sites**. The progression of tool styles provides **diagnostic** artifacts which may be cross-referenced to date sites. (Caution—Stone tool making can be dangerous, therefore, it is recommended that students be at least 12 years of age before attempting replication and must wear protective goggles and gloves.)

Materials: See audio visuals list in Appendix for demonstration film
A flint knapper or film
Diagrams and drawings

References: Hester (1980)
Montgomery (1985)
Shafer (1986)
Turner and Hester (1985)

Procedures: (1) Introduce tool making through live or filmed demonstrations. Show the series of steps in creating a tool as it is made or in drawings.
(2) Use a set of tools (or illustrations) which show a variety of tools. Ask students to propose how particular tools may have functioned. Point out that some information may be missing when you find the tools, for example, wooden part of tool. Show comparative tools used by recent people.
(3) Discuss the importance of tools as diagnostic artifacts—time markers.

Vocabulary: artifacts
diagnostic

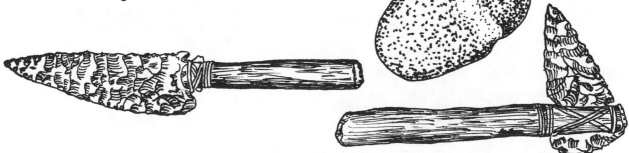

Analysis ★

Activity: Tools and Utensils or "What could I use this for?"

Levels: Grades 5-8

Objectives: The student will demonstrate an awareness of how function and material influence the
              structure, shape, and appearance of a tool.

PREPARATION:

Background: Native Americans utilized resources such as wood, bone, stone, and shell to make tools
              and utensils. The material, its natural shape or structure, determined how it would be used.
              A broken shell might be used as a scoop or a scraper. Stones might be used for hammers
              or net weights. Sometimes one resource was used as a tool to make another tool, such
              as an antler tip pressure-flaking tool used in the making of a projectile point.

Materials: Photographs or drawings of artifacts of stone, bone, and shell
              Tools and utensils from home, garage, or school
              Drawing paper
              Pen or pencils

References: Turner and Hester (1985)

Procedure: (1) Students will select and draw an artifact. Students might be encouraged to use a grid
                   system to redraw photographs or drawings so that proportions are accurate.
              (2) The student will decide for what the tool might have been used. This determination
                   will be based upon the shape and structure as well as the raw material itself.
              (3) From the tools and utensils available, the students will select and draw a contempo-
                   rary tool that is used in the same way. The artifact and present-day tool or utensil
                   will have similar functions.

Extension: (1) Reverse the procedure, selecting a present-day tool to draw and an artifact which
                   would perform a similar function.
              (2) Students may write a paragraph explaining the factors considered in making
                   choices to match up artifacts with tool or utensil.

Activities: Pottery

Levels: Grades 3-8

Subjects: Fine Arts, Social Studies

Objectives: Students will (1) study pottery from specific **cultures,** (2) create a **vessel,** and (3) learn how archeologists analyze pot **sherds.**

PREPARATION:

Background: Vessels often indicate use or function depending on the shape. This is important as archeologists develop a story of how the people lived at a site. Decoration of pottery can also tell us about the people. Motifs sometimes provide clues to significant elements of the environment and/or beliefs.

Materials: Clay (re-wedged or even self-drying simplify preparation)
Books with examples of pottery of the culture studied

References: Baylor (1972)
Glubok (1964)
Minor (1972)
Montgomery (1985)
Shafer (1986)

Procedures: *Directions for making a pinch pot:*
(1) Knead clay and shape into a ball about the size of a fist.
(2) Plunge thumb into the center of the ball.
(3) Gently press up and out with the thumb.
(4) Smooth the exterior wall from the outside with the finger.
(5) Decorate with design.
(6) Dry thoroughly (2 to 3 days) then fire.

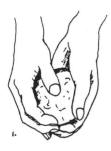
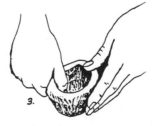
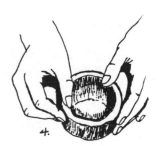
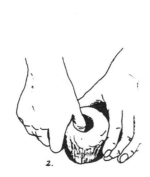

Directions for making a coiled pot:

(1) Knead the clay then take a portion to shape into cigar shape; roll this portion back and forth under the palms of the hands on a level surface to make a coil.
(2) Using coils, form a base.
(3) Shape a flat (pancake-like) base.
(4) Attach coils firmly, one at a time to the base.
(5) Coils may be pinched together as the pot is built and then scraped on the exterior and interior to alter the shape and smooth the sides.
(6) Decorate with special motifs.
(7) Allow pottery to dry completely. Fire the pot, if practical.

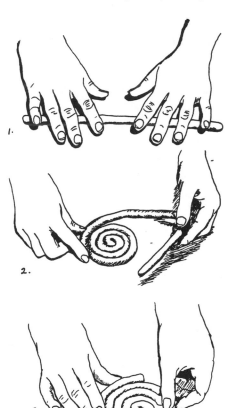

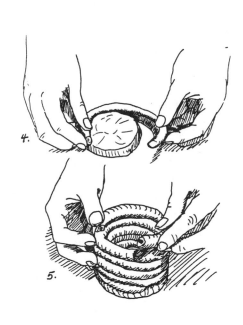

Extension: When making the pots have each student create two so that one may be broken as part of the study. Have students fracture their pot and pass only a few sherds on to another student to reconstruct.

Vocabulary: culture
sherd
vessel

Activities

Activity: Flotation

Levels: Grades 5-8

Subjects: Language Arts, Science, Social Studies

Objectives: The students will (1) practice classification and (2) describe ways of satisfying basic
                needs.

PREPARATION:

Background: Students will be given the opportunity to practice lab techniques used by archeologists.
             They will be able to recover cultural or biological remains from soil, identify, classify,
             and interpret those remains. Fine **screening** is an important technique in recovering
             material which would be lost without this process.

Materials: Buckets or basins with water
             Nylon stockings to serve as sieves
             Soil with small items, including seeds and shells
             Bags for materials after sorting
             Comparative pictures for identification of finds

References: Hole, Heizer, and Graham (1965)

Procedures: (1) Discuss the value of **flotation** for finding very small artifacts and floral materials.
              (2) Divide the students into work groups. Direct them to fill the stockings with about a
                   cup of soil; immerse the dirt in water until the dirt has percolated out and only small
                   items remain. These should be spread on paper to dry.
              (3) Have students sort the material into categories and create a catalog sheet to reflect
                   the remains.
              (4) Have student draw conclusions about the **subsistence** and activity patterns of the
                   people who lived at the "site".

Vocabulary: flotation
              screening
              subsistence

Analysis ★ ▬▬▬▬▬▬▬▬▬▬▬▬▬▬▬▬▬▬▬▬▬▬▬▬

Activity: Preservation of Materials

Levels: Grades 3-8

Subjects: Language Arts, Social Studies, Science

Objectives: The students will (1) arrange ideas and information, (2) predict outcome, (3) identify customs, and (4) describe changes in the individual and society.

PREPARATION:

Backgound: Archeologists are able to analyze only those objects which remain over time. Therefore, there are often events or happenings which are not be reflected in the archeological record. This exercise will encourage students to recognize the benefits and limitations of archeological investigations.

Materials: Unlined paper
              Pencil
              Ruler or straight edge

References: Fagan (1978)
              Macaulay (1979)
              Nichols (1988)

Procedures: (1) Discuss degrees of preservation at archeological sites. Extremes of dampness, cold, or dryness generally provide the best conditions for preservation.
              (2) Divide the class into study groups and assign the following "sites" for consideration:
                  kitchen of a house
                  student's room
                  den of house
                  football stadium
                  classroom
                  restaurant
              (3) Instruct the students to list or draw items they think will last until A.D. 3000. (Older students may draw a map of the site today and one showing the site in A.D. 3000.)
              (4) Have a spokesperson from each group report as if he were an archeologist in A.D. 3000. How would the site be interpreted in A.D. 3000?
              (5) Conclude with a discussion of what archeologists can and cannot determine from the artifactual evidence.

Activity: A Class in a Box

Levels: Grades 3-8

Subjects: Language Arts, Social Studies, Science

Objectives: The students will (1) identify local (class) traditions and customs, (2) predict outcome
                 and generalize, and (3) draw logical inferences.

PREPARATION:

Background: Archeologists learn about people by studying the materials (**artifacts**) found in the sites.
            What would early people have left if they knew archeologists would be interested? By
            having students bring an object you may develop a composite of the class "**culture.**" Is
            there a pattern or common theme?

Materials: One small item from each student and a shoe box

Procedures: (1) Ask students to bring an item to school which would tell about themselves. Have
                     them put the objects into a shoe box without looking.
                 (2) Have students consider the assemblage by saying: Pretend you are archeologists in
                     the year A.D. 4000. You have just excavated these items as artifacts from a site.
                     What can you tell about these people and their way of life? Try to organize the
                     responses into categories: food, clothing, shelter, tools, utensils, status, and aesthet-
                     ics.

Vocabulary: artifact
                 culture

Interpretation ★★ ▬▬▬▬▬▬▬▬▬▬▬▬▬▬▬▬▬▬▬▬▬▬▬▬

Activity: Time Capsule

Levels: Grades 3-8

Subjects: Language Arts, Social Studies, Science

Objectives: The students will (1) identify local traditions and customs, (2) describe ways a community satisfies its needs, (3) arrange ideas and information, and (4) form generalized statements.

PREPARATION:

Background: The information archeologists have to work with comes primarily from an artifact **assemblage** - that is, the collection of **artifacts** from a **site**. These artifacts can be classified according to information which they can yield. Categories used for this classification include: shelter, food, clothing, tools, pottery, weapons, government, religion, art, and aesthetics.

Materials: Paper on which to list "artifacts" considered important

References: Field (1989)
              Hester (1980)
              Newcomb (1961)

Procedures: (1) Tell students that they will have the opportunity to develop a set of artifacts which will tell future archeologists about the United States today.
              (2) Divide the class into several groups (5 to 7 in a group). Have each group select 10 artifacts (objects made or modified by man) which would give information about America today. Each group should list these artifacts and relate what they will tell about our life.
              (3) Bring the groups together and have each share their list. List all artifacts on the board then have the class vote on the 10 that tell the most. What is the picture of American life based on these artifacts? Is anything left out or missing?

Vocabulary: artifacts
              assemblage
              sites

Activity: Misinterpretations

Levels: Grades 6-8

Subjects: Language Arts, Social Studies, Science

Objectives: The student will (1) identify local customs, (2) distinguish between fact and opinion, (3) develop logical inferences, and (4) expand on topic.

PREPARATION:

Background: Archeologists must often use an educated guess to determine **function** of **artifacts** found. They compare the artifacts to known objects and to records showing ancient objects. Even with the best research the use of some artifacts is hypothetical. There are several fanciful accounts which will set the stage for this lesson.

Materials: Paper for lists or drawings
Optional - antique tools which are not common for students to guess the function
(Pictures from old catalogs can also be used here.)

References: Macaulay (1979)
Nathan (1974)
Spradley (1975)
Weitzman (1975)

Procedures: (1) Explain how archeologists sometimes must infer use or function of artifacts without proof. Discuss some possible antique tools, display them, and let students guess their function. (Pictures from old catalogs can also be used for interest.)
                (2) Have students consider how an archeologist will explain the following objects 500 years from now: tennis racket, microwave oven, roller skates, plus others added by the students.

Extension: Are we imposing ideas from our culture on those which we investigate?

Vocabulary: artifact
                function

Interpretation ★ ━━━━━━━━━━━━━━━━━━━━━━━━━━━━━━━━━━━━

Activity: Dating Materials

Levels: Grades 6-12

Subjects: Language Arts, Science, Social Studies

Objectives: The student will (1) research technical **dating** procedures and (2) report on them in class.

┌───┐
PREPARATION:

Background: Archeologists call on many scientists and technicians to analyze their findings. Dates and time periods are very important in interpretation of sites. Therefore, expenses must be budgeted for those special tests in order to validate the investigation.

References: Cork and Reid (1984)
             Hester, Heizer, and Graham (1975)
             McHargue and Roberts (1977)
└───┘

Procedures: (1) Have each student select a topic from the following dating techniques:

        potassium argon   radiocarbon (C14)
        fission tracking   thermoluminescence
        dendrochronology   archeomagnetic determination
        obsidian hydration

Since these topics are very technical, a librarian's assistance may be needed to locate good references.

(2) Ask the students to prepare a report with a visual aid (poster) including the following information:
    a. Name of technique
    b. Process of testing
    c. Materials which may be tested
    d. Special handling required
    e. Artifacts usually tested
    f. Special interpretation
    g. Limit of accuracy

Activity: Carbon 14 Dating

Levels: Grades 6-8

Subjects: Language Arts, Science

Objectives: The students will (1) learn about technical procedures and (2) use classification skills.

PREPARATION:

Background: All living organisms absorb C14 while they are alive. Once an organism dies it loses C14 at a fixed rate. Therefore, by measuring the disintegration rate of C14, scientists can determine the date an organism died. Remember, only materials that were once alive can be dated by the C14 method. This method destroys the specimen.

Materials: References on dating techniques
             Paper for chart or written work

References: Cork and Reid (1984)
             Fagan (1978)
             Hester, Heizer, and Graham (1975)
             Nicholas (1988)

Procedures: (1) Explain the theory of C14 to the students. (See Interpretation, Section I.)
             (2) Have the students classify the following artifacts as datable by C14 methods or not datable by C14 methods.

papyrus scrolls	bone tool
metal hammer	wooden bowl
linen cloth	stone statue
ceramic vessel	oyster shell

Teacher Key: *Not* datable by C14
             metal hammer
             ceramic vessel
             stone statue

Interpretation ★ ▬▬▬▬▬▬▬▬▬▬▬▬▬▬▬▬▬▬▬▬▬▬▬▬▬▬▬▬▬▬▬▬

Activity: Dendrochronology (Tree-ring Dating)

Levels: Grades 3-8

Subjects: Language Arts, Social Studies, Science

Objectives: The students will (1) elaborate and use description, (2) acquire data through the senses, and (3) make and interpret time-lines.

PREPARATION:

Background: Charts have been developed for certain trees which show patterns of growth rings. These rings can be counted and analyzed. Tree rings are often visible in boards, rafters, lintels, and facings. Sometimes samples from these pieces of wood can be matched to a chart with dates to determine when the wood was cut and, therefore, how old it is.

Materials: Cross sections of trees from wood sold for fireplaces, (optional) magnifying glass

References: Cork and Reid (1984)
Fagan (1978)
Hester, Heizer and Graham (1975)
Nichols (1988)

Procedures: (1) Explain the process of **dendrochronology** to the students. (See Interpretation, in Section I.)
(2) Distribute tree sections to the students. Tell the students to assume that the sections are freshly cut.
(3) Ask students to count the rings in the cut to determine the age of the tree when it was cut. Have each student draw a diagram of the rings they see.
(4) Have students arrange the cuts in order from youngest to oldest.

Extension: Ask the students to imagine finding a piece of wood that could be dated in an excavation. Have them describe finding it, tell what its use was and what other artifacts were associated with it.

Vocabulary: dendrochronology

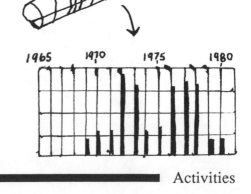

Activity: Chronological Sequence

Levels: Grades 3-8

Subjects: Language Arts, Social Studies, Science, Fine Arts

Objectives: The students will (1) show an awareness and sensitivity to the man-made environment, (2) arrange ideas and information in sequence, (3) draw logical inferences, and (4) use classifying skills.

PREPARATION:

Background: In analyzing **artifacts**, charts are developed which arrange artifacts in **chronological** sequence. This means recognizing style changes over time. Once a chart has been developed for a class of artifacts (i.e. pottery, projectile points, nails, etc.) a single artifact can be matched to the chart and given the estimated date. While chronological sequencing sounds complicated, we use it daily in recognizing the ages of styles (cars, bicycles, dress, etc.). It is exciting for students to see that they can place items in sequence and use that information to establish a date.

Materials: A chart or poster which relates some objects in chronological order. (Many texts on classical sites show pottery charts.)

References: Fagan (1978)
                 Hester (1980)
                 Nichols (1988)
                 Weitzman (1975)

Procedures: (1) Discuss with students the importance of knowing the "age" of artifacts - to place them in proper perspective, to appreciate their antiquity, etc.
                 (2) Show the students a chart which has been developed to show chronology of an object, such as cars, bicycles, pottery, or tombstones.
                 (3) Ask how they make this kind of evaluation daily based on style.
                 (4) Have students develop a topology chart for objects. Many objects lend themselves to this type of sequence. (clothes, cars, lighting, etc.)
                 (5) Let students relate their chart to the class and then have the class "date" one of the objects. Sometimes you can not designate a specific year for an object. You can only say it was after "x" and before "y".

Vocabulary: artifact
                 chronology

Name _____   Date _____

CHRONOLOGICAL SEQUENCE

View the bicycles and number them in chronological sequence (4 = oldest, 1 = most recent).
Explain your answer.

Activity: Color the Artifacts

Levels: Grades 5-8

Subjects: Social Studies, Science, Language Arts

Objectives: The students will (1) recognize and (2) identify artifacts.

PREPARATION:

Background: Distinguishing between natural objects (**ecofacts**) and objects made by humans (**artifacts**) is an important task of the archeologists. This lesson would put the students in the role of archeologist to classify objects and identify their use.

Materials: Drawings showing an Indian campsite and the interior of a pioneer homestead.

References: Vander-Meulen (1983)
            Warren (1971)
            Zappler and Simons (1984)

Procedures: (1) Discuss the meanings of artifact and ecofact with the students. Solicit examples.
            (2) Pass out the Activity Sheets. Have students identify potential artifacts and ecofacts. Have them color the artifacts and mark ecofacts with an E.

Vocabulary: artifact
            ecofact

Name _____ Date _____

COLOR THE ARTIFACTS

Color the artifacts in the pictures. Mark ecofacts with an E.

Activity: If You Were An Indian

Levels: Grades 3-8

Subjects: Language Arts, Social Studies, Fine Arts

Objectives: The students will (1) develop skills in writing, (2) show an understanding of others, (3) describe ways of providing for basic needs, and (4) express themselves through art.

PREPARATION:

Background: After studying various tribes and lifeways, discuss with the students what life would be like as an Indian.

Materials: Notebook or paper for writing
              Materials for sketching or drawing a mural

References: Campbell (1976)
              Newcomb (1961)
              Shafer (1986)
              Warren (1971)

Procedures: Have students answer the following questions. If you were an Indian:
1)   where would you live,
2)   to what tribe would you belong,
3)   what would you wear,
4)   what would you eat,
5)   what would your duties be,
6)   who would be your enemies,
7)   how would you protect yourself,
8)   what would be your religious beliefs?

These may be answered in statement form, as a diary, with a series of drawings, or on a mural.

Interpretation ★ ▬▬▬▬▬▬▬▬▬▬▬▬▬▬▬▬▬▬▬▬▬▬▬▬

Activity: Imagine Living in Ancient Times

Levels: Grades 3-8

Subjects: Language Arts, Social Studies, Science, Health, Fine Arts

Objectives: The students will (1) use comprehension skills to gain meaning, (2) gain experience in communicating data, (3) describe ways a community satisfies needs for food, clothing, shelter, and (4) learn what affects the well-being of people collectively.

PREPARATION:

Background: As archeologists study the results of their investigation they ask the question - how did the inhabitants satisfy their needs ?

Materials: An account of prehistoric life, Spanish expedition, or an early homesteader which would relate details of environment
The summary chapter of an archeological report

References: Auel (1985)
Newcomb (1961)
Shafer (1986)

Procedures: (1) Ask students to pretend that they have been teleported to another time period in a specific area, for example, the Archaic, 6,000 B.C. in the Trans-Pecos.
               (2) Read information on the environment and resources to them. Have them recount what they know of the skills of the early people of that area. Brainstorm and make a list for easy reference.
               (3) Ask them to relate in skits (drama) or on a mural (art) how they would adapt. What skills do they have that would be useful in an earlier time (universal characteristics)?

Extension: Reverse the situation. How would an Archaic hunter adapt in our twentieth century world?

Teacher Key: Some skills needed by early people—
               tool making
               weaving (basketry)
               tracking animals

Activity: Contact Episode

Levels: Grades 3-8

Subjects: Language Arts, Social Studies, Fine Arts

Objectives: The students will (1) elaborate and expand upon themes, (2) develop appreciation of others, (3) show expression through art or drama, and (4) recognize different viewpoints.

PREPARATION:

Background: The first contact with European explorers or missionaries must have been frightening to the Indians in America. Some journals and logs relate the impressions of the Spanish and the French. A few written accounts tell of the Indian reactions. Another episode might be "contact" with a river boat or locomotive.

Materials: Notebook or paper for writing OR art materials for drawing

References: Goble (1987)
             Zappler and Simons (1984)
             Newcomb (1961)

Procedures: (1) Read several accounts of contact between Indians and explorers or early settlers.
             (2) Have students write, draw, or dramatize a fictional account of the arrival of the explorers and missionaries. Be sure that both the Indian and European view points are included.
             (3) Have the students share their work with each other.

Extension: What artifacts would be found to document such an encounter? Have students list those objects which would remain as evidence of the episode. Also consider what is not left for the archeological record.

Interpretation ★ ▬▬▬▬▬▬▬▬▬▬▬▬▬▬▬▬

Activity: Future Archeology

Levels: Grades 3-8

Subjects: Language Arts, Social Studies, Science, Fine Arts

Objectives: The students will (1) show an awareness to the man-made environment, (2) describe how individuals change over time, (3) predict outcomes, and (4) elaborate and use description to inform.

PREPARATION:

Background: When archeological sites are found there are often voids in the record, i.e. many objects have disintegrated. The lack of specific information means that sometimes there are questions left unanswered. The following exercise will help students understand this deficiency.

Materials: Paper for a list or drawing

References: Fagan (1978)
              Macaulay (1979)
              Nathan (1974)
              Nichols (1988)

Procedures: (1) Relate the following scenario to the class :
                  It is A.D. 3000 and archeologists from a distant planet have landed on earth. They want to discover what life was like 1000 years earlier. They come to the ruins of your home and begin to excavate your room.
              (2) Answer the following questions about what archeologists would find to tell them about you:
                  — What objects would remain?
                  — What things would they think were important to you? Is this accurate?
                  — How did you live? Did you have many objects that let you live comfortably? Shelter? Heat? Light? Plumbing?
                  — Could they tell what you really do every day? Could the archeologists determine your religion? Could they tell the form of government we have?

Extension: What objects would you leave in a time capsule to tell about yourself?

Activity: Design a Tomb: Supplies for an Afterlife

Levels: Grades 5-8

Subjects: Language Arts, Social Studies, Fine Arts

PREPARATION:

Background: Archeologists often find significant **artifacts associated** with burials. Many ancient people believed in a physical afterlife and, therefore, buried objects that they thought the deceased would need.

Materials: References showing important tomb discoveries (King Tutankhamen, etc.)
              Writing or drawing supplies

References: Fagan (1985)
              Grosvenor (1974)
              Macaulay (1979)

Procedures: (1) Have students list the objects that they or a specific profession might want to have buried with them. Possible professions include doctor, artist, teacher, farmer, purveyor, and engineer.
              (2) Have each student draw a picture of the tomb, as if the **custom** of burying objects with the dead were followed.
              (3) Ask each student to share and explain his or her representation of a tomb with the class.

Vocabulary: artifact
              associated
              custom

Replication ★★

Activity: Games Played by Native Americans

Levels: Grades 3-8

Subjects: Language Arts, Social Studies, Physical Education

Objectives: The student will (1) recognize leisure activities which move across cultural boundaries
                 and (2) participate in a group activity.

PREPARATION:

Background: Many games were played by the Native Americans. They played active games similar to
              soccer, lacrosse, and kickball. Guessing games and dice games were also popular. When
              game pieces are found in excavation, we know that people had time to entertain them-
              selves with leisure activities.

Materials: Sticks, acorns, shells, or rocks painted on one side

References: Culin (1975)

Procedures: One dice game is easily prepared and played by two people.
                  (1) Using game pieces painted on one side, each person chooses a color.
                  (2) The dice are cast with players taking turns. A player wins points equal to his
                      color showing each time the dice are thrown.
                  (3) Set a goal (number of points) so that there is a stopping point.

Activity: Comparing Supermarkets

Levels: Grade 3-8

Subjects: Social Studies, Science, Language Arts, Health

Objectives: The student will use reference materials to discover how **prehistoric** people utilized their environment to provide for their needs.

PREPARATION:

Background: Archeological research and **ethnological** information often combine to give us a sense of how prehistoric people fed themselves.

Materials: Paper for chart

References: Aliki (1976)
Kimball (1965)
Newcomb (1961)
Shafer (1986)
Vander-Meulen (1983)
Zappler and Simons (1984)

Procedures: (1) Have students investigate what prehistoric people ate. Significant information has been found in dry caves which have good preservation of materials. At most sites, only items such as bone fragments, shells, nutshells, and seeds remain.

(2) Have students make a chart showing items from present day supermarkets and their prehistoric correlates. Compare the wide range of materials available in today's supermarket (tools, clothing, and school supplies) to the resources of the prehistoric people.

Extension 1:   Bring prehistoric "snacks" to taste and to illustrate the types of preservation essential for prehistoric people.

Extension 2:   Divide students into three groups and have them plan menus for (a) a cafeteria lunch, (b) fast-food meal, and (c) birthday dinner for the family. Have them predict which remains will survive as evidence for archeologists of the future to find. What conclusions would they develop regarding our diet? What about today's packaging and utensils?

Vocabulary: ethnology
prehistoric

ACTIVITY SHEET

Name ______________________________ Date ______________

COMPARING SUPERMARKETS

After reading about the diet and eating habits of prehistoric people, see if you can compare modern day supermarkets with the environmental supermarket of the prehistoric people. Complete the following chart.

MODERN	**PREHISTORIC**
A. Produce	A. Produce
B. Meats	B. Meats
C. Drinks	C. Drinks
D. Utensils	D. Utensils
E. Other	E. Other

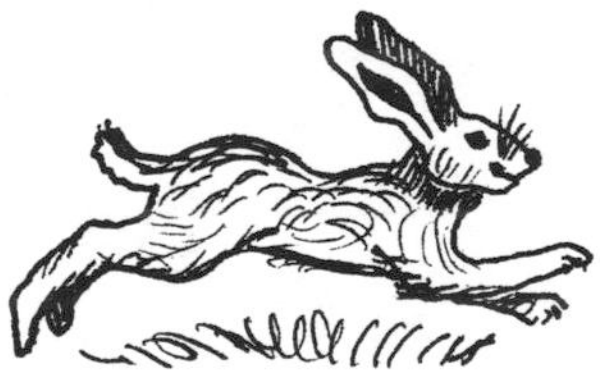

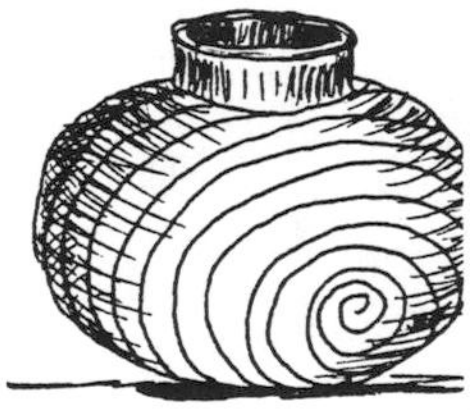

Activity: Farming and Gardening

Levels: Grade 3-8

Subjects: Science, Social Studies

Objectives: The student will (1) learn about plants and **cultivation** and (2) recognize the sources of food
                for early people.

PREPARATION:

Background: All food crops were started from native plants which where cultivated by people. Culti-
             vation of crops marks an important step in the culture and living standards of a people.
             With crops people often develop settlements and abandon their transitory **migrations**.

Materials: Garden area or window
             Tools
             Seeds or plants

References: Caduto (1988)
             Kimball (1965)

Procedures: (1) Have students investigate what prehistoric people ate. Significant information has
                 been found in dry caves which have good preservation of materials. At most sites,
                 only items such as bone fragments, shells, nutshells, and seeds remain.
             (2) Have students help prepare a garden area. Be sure to have good drainage and plant
                 the seeds or seedlings.
             (3) Keep careful records of weather, care, and growth of plants.
             (4) Harvest crops as they mature and enjoy a Native American feast.

Vocabulary: cultivate
             migrate

Replication ★ ▬▬▬▬▬▬▬▬▬▬▬▬▬▬▬▬▬▬▬▬▬▬▬▬▬▬▬▬▬▬

Activity: Forms of Shelter

Levels: Grades 3-8

Subjects: Social Studies, Art, Science

Objective: The student will (1) learn ways a community satisfies its need for shelter, (2) demonstrate
              ideas through art materials, and (3) gain experience in communicating data.

PREPARATION:

Background: Data illustrate how needs for **shelter** are associated with the lifestyle of a particular
              group. **Nomadic** hunting and gathering groups are associated with ephemeral shelters,
              often of brush. A settled life based on farming requires more permanent construction.
              The Plains Indians used tipis which were the ideal portable camping tent. European
              contact brought some Indian groups into the mission complex.

References: Grosvenor (1974)
              La Farge (1960)
              Newcomb (1961)
              Vander-Meulen (1983)
              Zappler and Simons (1984)

Procedures: (1) Divide the students into several groups so that each group can research a different style
                  of dwelling.
              (2) Once information has been found and studied, have the students fabricate a shelter.
                  Construction may be small models or life-size replicas.
              (3) Ask students to explain the background and construction methods for each shelter.

Extension: Suggest that students research the importance of the dome concept in construction. Have
              them build a dome from tooth picks.

Vocabulary: nomadic
              shelter

Some kinds of Indian shelter

Replication ★ ▬▬▬▬▬▬▬▬▬▬▬▬▬▬▬▬▬▬▬▬▬

Activity: Animal Hides

Levels: Grades 3-8

Subjects: Fine Arts, Social Studies

Objectives: The students will (1) study a variety of products made from animal hides, (2) discover
                 how efficiently peoples utilized their resources, (3) consider motifs as decorative and/or
                 symbolic elements, (4) create a **replica** of an item made from hide, and (5) demonstrate
                 inventive and imaginative expression through art materials.

PREPARATION:

Background: Indians used their resources economically, taking animals in the hunt which yielded
             hides that could function as clothing, shelter, and containers. Even the smallest strips of
             hide were saved and used for fringe and lacing. Usually women made these items,
             although men constructed some items of ceremonial value such as war shields.

Materials: Hide, fabric, or paper (scraps of leather are often available from a leather or shoe shop)

References: Campbell (1976)
             Glubok (1964)
             La Farge (1960)
             Grosvenor (1974)
             Minor (1972)
             Montgomery (1985)

Procedures: (1) Using visual aides, illustrate various items of hide attributed to native American
                     groups. (A museum trip would be a very visual way to research.) Emphasize the
                     perspective held by Indian groups of using the products of nature in wise and non-
                     wasteful ways. Elicit responses from the students on items that they might know—
                     dress, moccasins, toys, or war shields. Point out the decoration used. Categorize the
                     designs used.
                (2) Have students create an item from hide, fabric, or paper. Feathers, paint, shells, and
                     beads may be used as decoration. Suggested items: cradleboard, pouch, or war
                     shield.

Vocabulary: replica

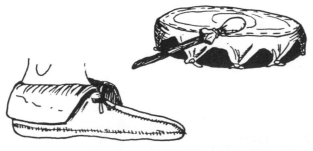

Activity: The Parfleche

Levels: Grades 5-8

Subjects: Social Studies, Fine Arts

Objectives: The student will demonstrate an awareness that one can create height, width, and depth with flat planes that are combined to make specific shapes.

PREPARATION:

Background: The "parfleche" was a rawhide case or folder used to carry clothing, food, or other articles. The Plains Indians used the simple geometric designs—diamonds, rectangles, triangles, squares—to decorate the luggage case. The design was painted in contrasting colors of red, black, yellow, and green. The hide was folded into a package and laced with leather thongs to keep the flaps closed. The parfleche was hung up, carried over the shoulder or attached to the saddle of a horse.

The word "parfleche" was used as early as 1700 to designate any article made of rawhide. Usually, the carrying case was rectangular square in shape and as large as 2 to 3 feet long.

Materials: Large brown grocery bags, canvas, cardboard, or leather 32" x 46"
Acrylic paint (or wax crayons if paper is used)
Leather thongs, cords, or string for lacing

References: Glubok (1972)
Minor, Marx (1972)
Montgomery (1985)
Salomon (1927)

Procedures: (1) Parfleche cases may be made from a variety of materials
    A. Cardboard or poster board pieces.
    B. Canvas or other fabric. Paint the outside light cream or gray.
    C. Brown paper or paper bags
        1) Soak bags in water about 10 minutes
        2) Loosen the glued seams and open bag
        3) Carefully squeeze out the water
        4) Spread paper out gently on newspaper to dry
        5) Glue dried bags together to form one strong bag.
(2) Cut parfleche as shown in the diagram.
(3) Fold along dotted lines.
(4) Unfold and punch holes as shown.
(5) Decorate the outside of the parfleche using crayons, color pencils, or paint.
(6) To close, fold top flap down first, then the bottom and sides.
(7) Lace string, yarn, or leather thongs through the holes to fasten the sides.

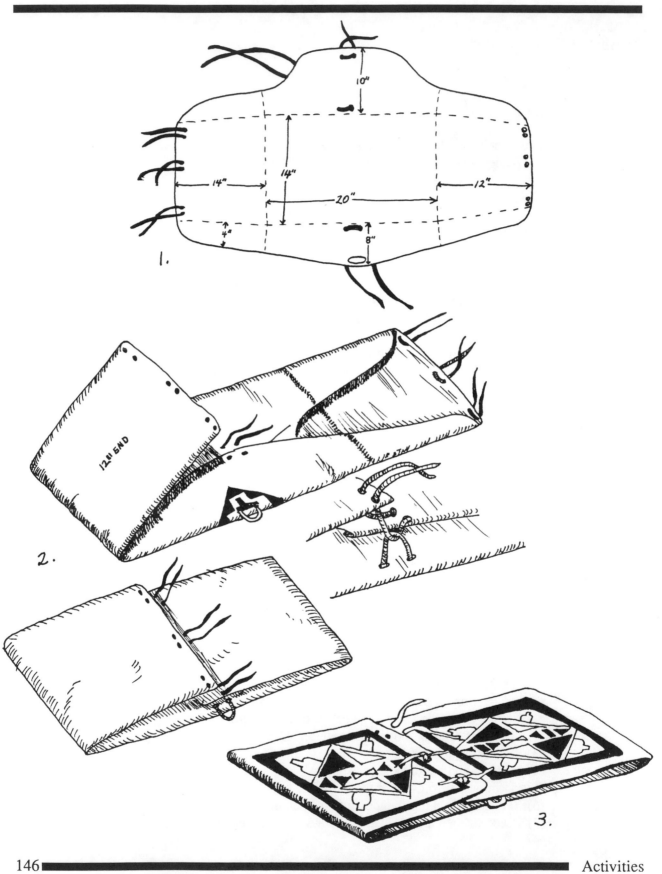

1.

2.

12" END

3.

Activity: Weaving

Levels: Grades 3-8

Subjects: Art, Social Studies

Objectives: The students will (1) identify specific **customs** and crafts used by early people and (2) demonstrate artistic expression by weaving.

PREPARATION:

Background: Native Americans used weaving skills to create mats, sandals, and nets as well as cloth and rugs. Early pioneers also did their own weaving.

Allow the topical emphasis of your unit to dictate the type of weaving and materials which you use.

Materials: Materials for weaving (paper strips, reeds, yarn, or string) often available at hobby shops

---

Procedures: (1) Show student **artifactual** materials which are woven.
(2) Demonstrate patterns and materials to use. If possible relate to unit of study.
(3) Have students work on individual projects.
(4) Display projects for everyone to see.

Vocabulary: artifact
custom

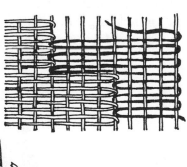

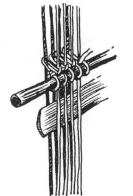

Replication ★

Activity: Early Graffiti: Painted Pebbles and Rock Art

Levels: Grades 3-12

Subjects: Fine Arts, Social Studies

Objectives: The student will (1) identify a specific art form, (2) use graphic sources to obtain information, and (3) demonstrate inventive and imaginative expression through art materials.

PREPARATION:

Background: Rock art and painted pebbles of the Lower Pecos show a tradition of painting that lasted thousands of years. Preserved because of the dry environment, the art includes paintings that are sometimes larger than life size on rockshelter walls, made up of human figures, animals, and other shapes. The smoothed river pebbles are small and portable and have black line paintings that are abstract or that seem to refer to human figures. The function of these art forms is not known, but it is believed that they could have been painted and used as part of rituals or ceremonies, perhaps for the Indians to insure special favors from the "spirit" world, such as a good hunt, or curing.

References: Jackson (1938)
Kirkland and Newcomb (1967)
Shafer (1986)

Procedures:
     (1)   Show illustrations of the rock art and pebble art from the Lower Pecos.
     (2)   Ask students to identify various elements in the paintings—plants, hunting, shapes, etc.
     (3)   Have the class create its own rock wall painting on brown paper, paint pebbles in the style of the Lower Pecos, or use designs of the students own creation. (Will archeologists centuries later understand designs by current students?)

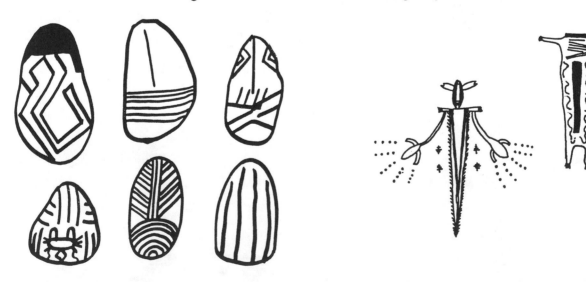

Activity: Picture Writing

Levels: Grades 3-8

Subjects: Fine Arts, Language Arts, Social Studies

Objectives: The students will (1) identify specific customs, (2) interpret legends, (3) use graphic
                 sources for information, and (4) use picture writing to create a story.

PREPARATION:

Background: Native American groups used pictures in numerous ways to relate events and teach
customs.

Materials: Paper for picture writing.

References: Campbell (1976)
             Grosvenor (1974)
             La Farge (1960)
             Minor (1972)
             Pine (1957)

Procedures: (1) Show many examples of picture writing to the students. Ask them to "translate" the
                      stories and decode the messages. (A rebus might also provide good practice.)
                 (2) Have the students create their own story using Indian symbols.
                 (3) Exchange stories among the students and have them try to decipher the ideas of
                      another.

AFTER BEFORE BAD GOOD

ANTELOPE ARROWS BEAR ALIVE BEAR DEAD BEAVER BIRD TRACKS BLANKET BOW AND ARROW, WAR

BROTHERS BUFFALO CAMP CANOE CANOE WITH WARRIORS CORN CLEAR DAY CROW

DEER DAY DEER TRACKS EAT EAGLE EAGLE FISH GUN

GEESE ECLIPSE EAST FIRE FORT HUNGRY HIDDEN HORSE

HEAR HUNT HORSE TRACKS ISLAND KNIFE LIGHTNING LOG CABIN A LOT OF MEAT

MORNING MOUNTAIN MEDICINE MAN MAKING PEACE NIGHT PEACE PIPE POWER RIVER

RAIN RUN SUN SKY SPIRIT SMALL POX SNOW STRONG

SNAKE STARS SING STORMY SEE TALK TREE TURTLE

THREE DAYS THREE NIGHTS THREE YEARS TWENTY WINTER WIND WHIRLWIND WAR

Some examples of picture writing

Activity: Winter Count

Levels: Grades 3-8

Subjects: Language Arts, Fine Arts, Social Studies

Objectives: The students will (1) identify specific customs, (2) interpret legends or keys, (3) interpret
              and make time-lines, (4) use graphic sources to obtain information, and (5) demonstrate
              inventive and imaginative expression through art materials.

PREPARATION:

Background: The Winter Count was a calendar kept by a tribe. Each year one important event was
           described and a symbol of the event was drawn on the smooth side of a buffalo hide.

Materials: An example of Winter Count; chart of symbols to use; hide, fabric, or paper

References: Campbell (1976)
            La Farge (1960)
            Grosvenor (1974)
            Minor (1972)
            Pine (1957)

Procedures: (1) "Read" the example of a winter count story.
              (2) Develop symbols to use in a contemporary story.
              (3) Have each student create his own Winter Count sheet. Each student will record one
                   important event for each year of his life by illustrating it in sequential order.
              (4) Share with the group as a culminating activity.

Sample Winter Count story which may be placed on hide (found on following page)

Name _____ Date _____

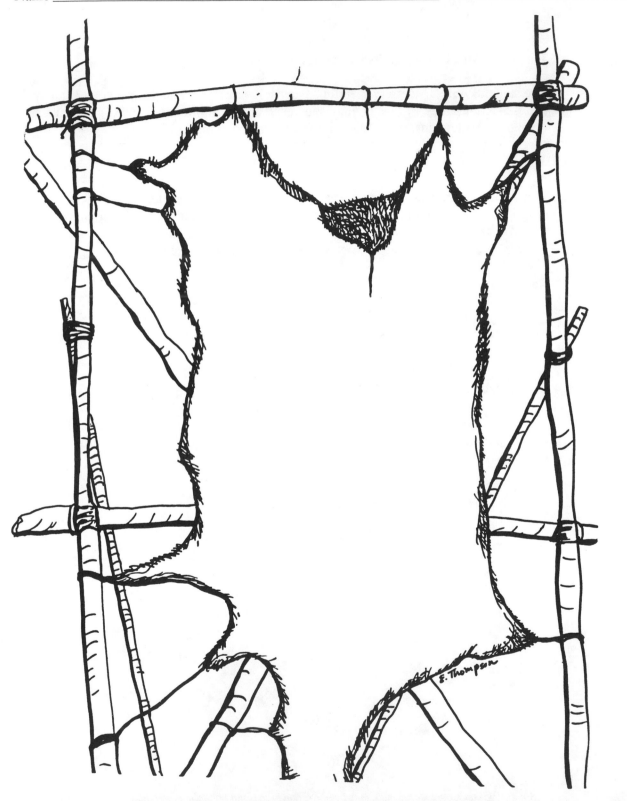

Activity: Music and Instruments

Levels: Grades 3-8

Subjects: Fine Arts, Social Studies

Objectives: The student will (1) develop an understanding and appreciation of self and others through musical cultures and heritage and (2) identify specific traditions, customs, and folkways.

PREPARATION:

Background: Rhythm or beat is the most important component of Indian music. Various instruments were used for rhythm with melody added occasionally. Instruments included drums, rattles, moraches (notched resonators), bull-roarers, flutes, and whistles.

Materials: Tape or record of traditional Indian music
             Materials to make instruments (see procedures)

References: Campbell (1976)
             Grosvenor (1974)
             La Farge (1960)
             Montgomery (1985)

Procedures: (1) Have students listen to music and identify instruments.
             (2) Have students make an instrument of their choice:
                  Drum—use round carton (chips, oatmeal, etc.); decorate with Indian symbols
                  Rattle—small container with pebbles, beans, and seeds
                  Flute—from cane or clay
                  Whistle—reed, wood, or bone
                  Morache—long stick with series of notches and shorter stick to draw across notches
                  Bull-roarer—flat piece of wood or bone; not more than 2" wide and 6" to 12" long attached to a cord at one end. Whirring sound is made by rotating the instrument overhead causing the roarer to spin.

             (3) Using the instruments, have students accompany the music on the tape or create their own song.

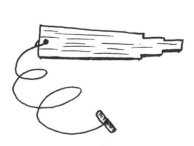   

Replication ★

Activity: Painting to Music

Levels: Grades 3-8

Subjects: Fine Arts, Social Studies

Objectives: The student will (1) use lines and shapes to create rhythm and motion and to lead the eye in certain directions, (2) create unity without monotony using repetition of shapes and lines in a painting, and (3) demonstrate an awareness of how artist's choices of media can limit or enlarge the eventual outcome of his creative activity. The decision to utilize a specific medium predetermines the eventual impact it will have.

PREPARATION:

Background: (1)   Do you know what rhythm and motion are? Motion is movement and movement with repetition can have rhythm. List things that have rhythm and motion.

heart beat	pistons inside an engine
drum beat	hopping
lightning	water/rain
Pac Man	objects in classroom
	rock dropped in water

          (2)   Talk about 4 specific types of rhythm.
              A) Repetitive: AAAA Hop, Hop, Hop, Hop
              B) Progressive: ABCD squatting to standing up
              C) Alternative: ABAB Hop, Jump, Hop, Jump
              D) Flowing: ABC, ABC Walking

              Have a student try to clap the above rhythms with their hands.
              Which type of rhythm is the "Wave" at a sports event?
              What are the different kinds of lines that can make rhythm? wavy, curved, straight, horizontal, vertical, diagonal, circles Rhythm or movement can be implied

          (3)   Have students take one of the types of rhythm and one kind of line and imply rhythm by drawing on paper.

          (4)   Talk about how the rhythm of repeating lines make the eye move in a certain direction. Hold up one of their drawings. "What is it in this picture that makes your eyes move in a certain direction (right, left, up, down)? Which of the 4 rhythms (progressive, alternative; flowing, repetitive) shows direction most? (Progressive)

          (5)   Ways to create Progressive Rhythm, to help lead the eye
              a) Large to small
              b) Light to dark
              c) Few to a lot
              d) Size variation
              e) Converging lines

---

page 1 of 2

(6)   What is the simplest picture you could make that would give the viewer some sort of feeling for direction and distance? Try on paper. Help students recognize that even when you have nothing more than two dots, distance and direction are implied.

One of the main reasons for <u>composition</u> in art is to <u>control</u> <u>the</u> <u>eye</u> <u>movement</u> <u>of</u> <u>those</u> <u>who</u> <u>look</u> <u>at the</u> <u>art.</u>

Procedures: 1)   Students are to listen to music and paint the beat as well as the melody. Suggestions for color schemes are:
- cool color for slow, sedate melody/beat
- warm colors for fast, aggressive song
- specific colors to the different types of rhythm.

For songs having different instruments or voices, assign a color to the instruments or voices.

2)   Have student use a variety of wet and dry painting media, such as tempera, watercolor, acrylic, or color pencils.

page 2 of 2

Reporting ★★

Activity: An Archeological Report

Levels: Grades 6-8

Subjects: Language Arts, Social Studies, Science

Objectives: The students will (1) understand the importance of reporting and (2) use guidelines to write a report.

PREPARATION:

Background: There are many suggested formats for reports. An outline of topics for a report is included in Procedures.

References: Hester (1980)
Hole and Heizer (1965)

Procedures:
(1) Have students work individually or as a team.
(2) Give students a copy (or put on board) of the outline for a report. Have them write a report using this format.

   I.   Introduction—Background and reasons for the investigation
       A. Site name and location on map
       B. Previous knowledge
       C. Aims and purpose
  II. Environment—Description
 III. Methodology—Procedures used
       A. Field Techniques
       B. Lab Techniques
 IV. Artifacts—Descriptive analysis
       A. Description in words
       B. Drawings or photographs
  V. Features—Associations with artifacts
 VI. Conclusion—Application of procedures
       A. Reconstruction of how people used the site
       B. Connections with other sites

Activity: In The News

Levels: Grades 3-8

Subjects: Language Arts, Social Studies, Science

Objectives: The students will (1) use a variety of sources for information and (2) distinguish between fact and opinion.

PREPARATION:

Background: Because ancient civilizations are often the subject of digs, students may not realize that archeologists are actively investigating sites today.

Materials: Articles from current magazines or newspapers
             Magazines in the appendix

References: Fagan (1985)
             Grosvenor (1974)

Procedures: (1) Have each student clip an article about archeology and bring it to class.
             (2) Have several students read their articles aloud.
             (3) Following each article, have the class discuss which statements were fact and which were opinion.

Extension: Encourage the students to put the articles on a bulletin board and locate each site on a map.

Activity: Famous Sites

Levels: Grades 5-8

Subjects: Language Arts, Social Studies, Science

Objectives: The students will (1) use graphic source for information and (2) use map skills to locate sites.

PREPARATION:

Background: Important archeological sites have been found all over the world. Many stories and articles have been written about those discoveries.

Materials: List of sites, atlas or map, blank map on which to locate sites

References: Fagan (1985)
             See Appendix for list of Audio Visuals

Procedures: (1) Have students locate at least six sites on a blank world map. Be sure to have good geographical information on the map - compass, scale, and legend.
              (2) Have students volunteer to research and present information about a site.

Extension: Have the students prepare a world map with the following famous sites.

Angkor, Cambodia   Tikal, Guatamala
Alta Mira, Spain   Troy, Turkey
Cahokia, MO   Williamsburg, VA
Chichen Itza, Mexico
Folsom, NM
Giza, Egypt
Jericho, Jordan
Knossos, Crete
Lascaux Cave, France
Luxor, Egypt
Machu Picchu, Peru
Olduvai Gorge, Tanzania
Ozette, WA
Palenque, Mexico
Plymouth, MA
Pompeii, Italy
Qumran, Jordan
Stonehenge, England
Sutton Hoo, England
Teotihuacan, Mexico

Activity: Share a Book

Levels: Grades 3-8

Subjects: Language Arts, Social Studies, Fine Arts

Objectives: The students will (1) develop skills in reading and writing, (2) express themselves
                  through art materials, and (3) identify traditions, customs, and folkways.

PREPARATION:

Background: Understanding the lives of Native Americans and early settlers helps the archeologists
             interpret the artifacts and features which are found.

References: A book or chapter about Native Americans or early settlers;
             See Juvenile Fiction in Appendix

Procedures: (1) Have students read a book or chapter in a book about Native Americans or early
                       settlers.
                  (2) Have each student share the information with the class by:
                       (a) making a poster of a scene
                       (b) creating a book marker about a character or scene
                       (c) drawing a mural
                       (d) writing a book report
                       (e) dramatizing a scene

Extension: Suggest each student identify what archeological remains would be found to indicate a
                  selected scene from the story.

Reporting ★

Activity: Spotlight on an Author

Levels: Grades 3-8

Subjects: Language Arts, Social Studies, Fine Arts

Objectives: The students will (1) review several works by the same author, (2) learn to recognize the style of a specific author, and (3) enjoy good literature.

PREPARATION:

Background: Numerous authors have specialized in writing about Native American life. The stories which have been written or retold by them greatly enrich our understanding of the culture. Works by two authors are listed for your consideration.

References:

Works by Byrd Baylor	**Works by Paul Goble**
And It Still Is That Way	*Beyond The Ridge*
Before You Came This Way	*Buffalo Woman*
The Desert Is Theirs	*Custer's Last Battle*
The Way to Start A Day	*Death of the Iron Horse*
They Put On Masks	*Lone Bull's Horse Raid*
When Clay Sings	*The Fetterman Fight*
	The Friendly Wolf
	The Gift of the Sacred Dog
	The Girl Who Loved Horses
	The Great Race
	Star Boy

Procedures:
    (1) Share several books by one author with the students. Talk about the author himself as well as his stories.
    (2) Have them draw a mural or act out a scene based on the story they like best.
    (3) Hold a contest to determine which of the stories was most popular. The students may campaign for their favorite story to try to convince others of its merit.

Activity: Fantasy Dig

Levels: Grades 3-8

Subjects: Language Arts, Social Studies, Science, Fine Arts

Objectives: The students will (1) elaborate ideas and expand topics, (2) make predictions, (3) iden-
               tify local traditions, folkways, and customs, and (4) demonstrate an awareness of the
               man-made environment.

PREPARATION:

Background: After reading about archeological investigation and excavation, students will probably
             have some ideas of their own. There are also some outlandish spoofs.

Materials: Paper or art supplies

References: Fagan (1985)
             Grosvenor (1974)
             Macaulay (1979)
             Nathan (1974)
             Spradley (1975)

Procedures: (1) Have students pretend that they are archeologists in search of a lost city or civiliza-
                    tion. Ask them to write a journal or play about this imaginary search.
               (2) Direct students to be very descriptive including comments on location, shelter, re-
                    sources, subsistence, trade, industry, government, and religion. Have them include
                    their impressions and interpretations.
               (3) Have students share their products with each other.

Reporting ★

Activity: Classroom Museum

Levels: Grades 3-8

Subjects: Language Arts, Social Studies, Science

Objectives: The students will (1) use visual aids to relate information, (2) use classification skills to organize data, and (3) identify customs and traditions.

PREPARATION:

Background: A final step in archeological reporting would ideally be an interpretive display or exhibit.

Materials: Objects (artifacts) brought to school or made in class to represent a specific cultural time period

---

Procedures: Have students bring artifacts to school (or make them) to illustrate a specific time period or culture. Arrange the artifacts in a display with interpretive labels. Have the students write a descriptive label and a label which explains how the object was used. Suggest that they relate themes of subsistence, social/government organization, religion, art, leisure, tools, and weapons.

Extension: This display could be set up in the school or neighborhood library or local mall.

Activity: Campaign for Conservation

Levels: Grades 3-8

Subjects: Language Arts, Social Studies, Science

Objectives: The students will (1) learn the value of protecting archeological sites, (2) prepare an ad–visual or oral–encouraging conservation, and (3) present their arguments to the class.

PREPARATION:

Background: It is estimated that 90% of the known sites on federal land in the Southwest have been disturbed. Underwater sites from the coast of Florida to the Channel Islands in California have been damaged or destroyed. National battlefield sites, from both the American Revolution and the Civil War, are endangered by looters and vandals. This limits the research efforts of archeologists. It is hoped that as people understand the value of archeology the sites will be protected.

Materials: Supplies to create an ad

References: Hester (1980)
             McHargue and Roberts (1977)
             Vander-Meulen (1983)

Procedures: (1) Discuss with students the value of archeological sites. Brainstorm for ideas about the ways archeology can enrich our lives. List these ideas on the board.
             (2) Relate incidents of looting and pot hunting that have destroyed valuable information.
             (3) Have the students work together in groups to plan a campaign against looters.
             (4) Have the students share their products—visually (by art projects) or orally (for example, speech, ad, or play).

Extension: Students may write:

             "Save the Past for the Future"
             Society for American Archeology
             Box 18364
             Washington, DC 20036

             The Archeological Conservancy
             415 Orchard Dr.
             Santa Fe, NM 87501

Name _____ Date _____

CAMPAIGN FOR CONSERVATION

There are a few simple rules for protecting archeological sites.

1. Do not dig in archeological sites without expert assistance. Discourage other people from digging in sites.
2. Do not pick up artifacts from sites. Discourage other people from picking up artifacts.
3. Do not buy, sell, or trade artifacts, because the trade in artifacts encourages other people to destroy sites.
4. Learn as much as possible about the Texas past. What you learn will help you identify and protect the sites and objects that are part of the unwritten history of Texas.
5. Join groups like the Texas Archeological Society, local archeological societies, and the Junior Historians. Groups like these try to learn about the past and why it is important to Texans of today.
6. Talk to other people about how important archeological sites are. Ask them to join you as a guardian of the Texas past.

- Adapted from Zappler and Simons (1984)

Create your own ad or cartoon encouraging conservation of archeological sites.

Activity: Bandelier

Levels: Grades 5-12

Subjects: Language Arts, Science, Social Studies

Objectives: Students will (1) demonstrate an understanding of issues involved in Cultural Resource Management, (2) explain problems involved in making decisions regarding cultural resources, (3) make decisions based on simulation, and (4) express an appreciation for the difficulty of making decisions when values and ethics are involved.

PREPARATION:

Background: Through participating in a simulation game, students will realize the problems involved in preserving our cultural heritage, a nonrenewable resource, and the role of Cultural Resource Management.

Materials: (Optional) Box of Props

Procedure:

The game of Bandelier requires at least two class periods with overnight preparation. Be sure the students understand the terms *simulation game* and *cultural resource management* before you begin.

The day before you plan to play the game, describe the problem faced by the residents of the town of Bandelier to the students. You may wish to give each student a copy of "The Situation" (following pages). Assign eight students the roles of individuals who will address the town council of Bandelier on the proposed archeological excavation. The remaining students will be the residents of Bandelier who will vote on the issue; they will be given the opportunity to participate in the discussion following individual presentations. Give each student chosen to play a major role a slip of paper with the name of his character and the opinion he holds. Members of the audience should receive the "Notes to Audience" sheet (following pages). You, the teacher, will play the role of the mayor of Bandelier, who acts as the moderator of the council.

Tell the students assigned major roles to prepare a 3-5 minute presentation of their character's position. Encourage them to be as expressive as possible. They may elaborate upon their character as much as they wish. For example, Jane Andrews might complain that involving the townspeople in the excavation would interfere with her research. Ms. Thompson might be a member of the Bandelier Garden Club, looking forward to landscaping the new park. One of the characters in favor of the park might introduce the rivalry with the neighboring town of Jennings. The students playing members of the audience should review the situation and begin thinking of possible solutions to the problem.

The next day, bring a box of props (optional) to class, e.g., a tin foil star for the chief of police, an oversized book for the school principal. Arrange chairs for the members of the panel facing the audience. As mayor, review the situation and introduce each participant, in the order in which they are listed. Other speakers and members of the audience are not permitted to ask questions or make comments during the presentations.

After the speakers have concluded their presentations, summarize the significant points briefly. Then open the floor for discussion. Members of the panel are permitted to take part. Members of the audience may question them, or they may simply state their own views. Encourage free debate. Allow 20-30 minutes for the discussion.

Following the discussion, write the proposed solutions to the problem on the blackboard. There should be at least four: the archeological excavation, the park, half-and-half, and "hands-off." Students may come up with other feasible alternatives (and some not so feasible.) Call for the vote. (Remember that the result of the vote is not important.) Students playing roles must vote according to their assigned character. Jane Andrews and Stephen Abernathy may not vote as they are not residents of Bandelier.

The Situation

The town council of Bandelier is planning to build a new park to celebrate the town's centennial next year. Practically everyone is in favor of the new park. Townspeople are especially eager that the park be even more beautiful than the one in the neighboring town of Jennings. An intense rivalry exists between the two towns.

Bandelier, population 5013, is located in the middle of the farm belt. The town is fairly prosperous because it serves as a central market for outlying potato districts. Bandelier is an old, established community. The residents are very proud of their small and friendly town and are determined that it will not lose its distinctive character.

The town owns a two-acre strip of property close to the downtown shopping area which would be an ideal location for the park. There is no other suitable location within the town's budget. The proposed site is a pretty area—it's slightly hilly and a small stream runs part way around the perimeter. It's only two blocks north of the Bandelier Savings and Loan and the Dairy Queen.

Local merchants and service organizations are quite excited about the project. A group of downtown businessmen has formed a "Spark Behind the Park" organization to help raise money. High school students have offered to contribute funds raised by candy sales and carwashes. The Bandelier Savings and Loan is sponsoring a contest to choose the best park logo from designs submitted by town residents. Bids have already been made for the construction contract.

However, last Friday an archeologist from the state university at Jennings spoke to a special meeting of the town council. She told the council that she believes there is a prehistoric Indian site in the middle of the proposed site for the new park. She exhibited a sizeable collection of pottery pieces and stone artifacts from the area to support this statement. Her findings and conclusions have been verified by the state archeologist's office. The archeologist is petitioning the town of Bandelier for permission to subject the site to a complete archeological analysis. She is certain that excavation of the site would contribute greatly to knowledge about the area's prehistoric inhabitants.

Members of the town council were very disturbed by this request. After a long debate, they voted to hold a public hearing on the proposed park construction. They have invited individuals representing various viewpoints to make presentations at the meeting. Following the presentations, residents of Bandelier will be asked to consider the various alternatives and register their preference. A simple majority is all that is necessary to make a binding decision, in most modern municipalities. (You may wish to alter the rules to reflect the decision-making procedure in many Indian communities, where a consensus must be reached before a matter is decided, so that there is no disgruntled minority.)

page 2 of 4

CHARACTER DESCRIPTIONS

JANE ANDREWS, Archeologist from Jennings State University:
Dr. Andrews discovered the site at the location of the proposed park. She wants to excavate it, analyze the findings, and publish the results. She believes that the new information will contribute greatly to knowledge about the area's prehistoric inhabitants.

SAM OWENS, Local Merchant:
Mr. Owens, who owns the local hardware store, was the organizer of the "Spark Behind the Park" group. He believes the park will add to the town's prestige in the county and help the town to grow more prosperous. Moreover, his son is a construction worker, and Mr. Owens is afraid the proposed excavation will take jobs away from Bandelier residents.

SARAH PETERS, Principal of Bandelier High School:
Ms. Peters regards the proposed archeological project as an unparalleled educational opportunity for the children of Bandelier. She thinks the students will learn a great deal from watching (or helping) the archeologists excavate the site. She believes the residents should not stand in the way of the opportunity to learn more about themselves and their past.

CARL POTTER, Chief of the Bandelier Police:
Chief Potter doesn't want the archeologists in town. He fears that the new ideas and different lifestyles of the university crowd will destroy the character of his "nice little town."

STEPHEN ABERNATHY, State Archeologist:
Dr. Abernathy wants the site left untouched, so that the cultural resources will be preserved until a workable plan for excavation and analysis can be developed by his office.

PAULA THOMPSON, President of the Elementary School PTA:
Ms. Thompson is in favor of the park because children in Bandelier need a safe place to play. She believes that an attractive, well-designed park would encourage family togetherness and be good for the community.

HOWARD SUSSMAN, President of the County Historical Society:
Mr. Sussman wants to encourage interest in local history. He suggests that the artifacts recovered from the excavation be displayed in a small museum to be established in Bandelier.

NOTES TO AUDIENCE

You will be given an opportunity to question the members of the panel following their presentations. You may wish to phrase your questions in the character of a resident of the town of Bandelier. Here are some examples:

—a retired homeowner whose land adjoins that of the proposed park. You wish neither park nor excavation because either invades your privacy.

—Mr. Owens' son, a construction worker. You are afraid you'll have to accept welfare if you don't get the job working on the park site.

—a member of the Garden Club. You are looking forward to landscaping the proposed park and have heard of some statewide contests in park landscape design in which Bandelier could compete.

—a local amateur archeologist. You are eager to share your knowledge of prehistory with the professional archeologists an excited about the possibility of learning more about the prehistory of the Bandelier area.

—a local merchant who has contributed a large sum to the "Spark Behind the Park" group. You threaten to withdraw this amount if the park project does not go through.

Use any of these or think up your own characters. Feel free to express your opinions (or those of your character) forcefully. When it comes time to vote, remember, compromises aren't always possible.

Suggestions for Discussion:

1. Ask individuals why they voted as they did. Was your mind made up from the beginning or did you change it? Who were the most convincing speakers?

2. Ask the students who played the roles of major characters for their reactions: Was your "gut" feeling different from your assigned role? Do you think you could have been more persuasive if you had a role you sympathized with?

3. Review dealing with ways sites are lost. Ask students how they can help preserve our state's past.

Extension: Each student writes a newspaper article summarizing the reasons for holding the hearing and the results of the vote; or each student chooses a character and in the identity of that character writes an editorial for the newspaper explaining his position.

Students can design posters to assist in site preservation, i.e. public awareness, legislation, or warning.

Source: *Studying the Prehistory of Man in Kentucky* (modified).

page 4 of 4

Activity: Archeology Awareness Week

Levels: Grades 3-8

Objectives: The students will (1) learn archeological terms, (2) become aware of the state's archeo-
                  logical heritage, and (3) participate in dissemination of information.

PREPARATION:

Background: In April, 1989, Archeology Awareness Week was initiated in Texas. Local archeologi-
             cal societies and museums mounted displays and sponsored seminars. The goal of the
             campaign is to increase awareness of archeology on a state-wide basis.

Materials: Supplies to make posters

Procedures: (1) Word for the Day: Select five words which carry concept meanings and introduce
                   one each day of the week.
              (2) Guest Archeologist: Invite an archeologist to talk regarding interesting sites. Have
                   the student prepare ahead of time by writing 3-5 questions each. Have the students
                   follow up with appropriate thank you notes.
              (3) Famous Sites: Pick five sites to discuss. Have students locate these on a map and
                   make a folder to keep information.
              (4) Posters: Have students draw posters to illustrate archeological methods. Display
                   them in the library or other central location to inform all students.

Extension: Write for additional information:

              Office of State Archeologist
              Texas Historical Commission
              Box 12276
              Austin, Texas 78711
              (512) 463-6090

              Texas Archeological Society
              Center for Archaeological Research
              U.T.S.A.
              San Antonio, Texas 78285

              Arizona Archaeology Week
              Archeological Assistance Program
              Technical Brief No. 2, October 1988
              U.S. Dept. of Interior
              Box 37127
              Washington, D.C. 20013-7127

Preservation ★ ▬▬▬▬▬▬▬▬▬▬▬▬▬▬▬▬▬▬▬▬▬▬▬▬▬

Activity: Design a Game

Levels: Grades 5-8

Subjects: Social Studies, Science, Language Arts

Objectives: The student will (1) review antiquities laws, (2) design a game about site protection, and
                 (3) share their game with classmates.

┌───┐
│ **PREPARATION:**   │
│   │
│ Background: Vandalism of archeological sites is increasing as commerical dealers destroy sites in │
│   order to make a profit selling objects. The looting of artifacts destroys information │
│   which could tell us about the past. It is reported that more money is spent buying illegal │
│   artifacts than is spent for research.   │
│   │
│ Materials: Materials for a board game   │
│   Parts for game-dice, markers, timer, etc.   │
│   │
│ References: Summary of the Antiquities Code of Texas (laws) in the Appendix   │
│   McHargue and Roberts (1977)   │
│   Vander-Meulen (1983)   │
│   Zappler and Simons (1984)   │
└───┘

Procedures: (1) Discuss with the students the value of archeological sites.
              (2) Review state and federal laws which apply to vandalizing archeological sites. See
                   the Antiquities Code of Texas in the Appendix.
              (3) Divide the students into teams to design a game about the current devastation. It
                   could be called "Go to Jail" or SOS (Save our Site) or other titles. Each game
                   should show at least five site types (chipping station, campsite, burial grounds,
                   ceremonial mound, food grinding, or bison kill) and two laws. It might also incor-
                   porate ideas for stewards or wardens who volunteer to work for protection of sites.

Name _____   Date

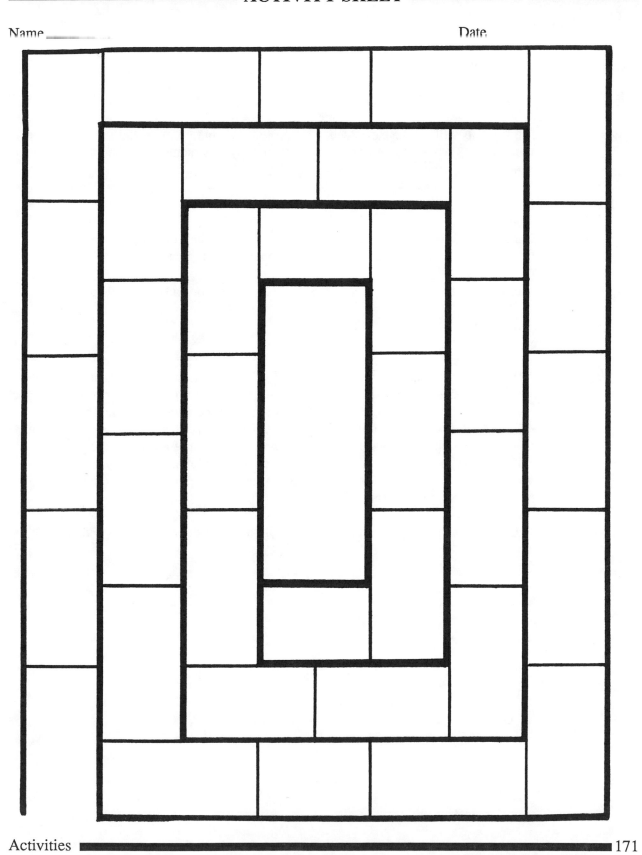

Activity: Interview an Archeologist

Levels: Grades 3-8

Subjects: Language Arts, Social Studies, Science, Fine Arts

Objectives: The students will (1) develop fluency in speaking, (2) obtain information from a variety of sources, (3) show expression through art, and (4) understand that individuals have the right to hold different view points.

PREPARATION:

Background: Students can learn about the archeological process and specific finds by interviewing an archeologist. They may also want to know about archeology as a career.

Materials: Locate a guest archeologist from a university, museum, or archeological society.

References: Hester (1980)
             Nichols (1988)

Procedures: **PRE-VISIT:** Announce that an archeologist will visit to talk about archeology. Share a biographical sketch, if possible. Ask each student to write down ten questions then select two to ask. Compare with classmates so that there will be a variety of questions.
PRESENTATION: Have one student introduce the speaker. After the speaker has made his or her presentation, have each student ask one question or more, if time permits.
POST-VISIT: Have students write a thank you letter or create a thank you artifact that would be meaningful to the speaker. Consider interests and incidents in the life of the archeologist in order to personalize the thank you.

Extension: Write SOPA (Society of Professional Archeologists) for their guidelines and code of conduct.

SOPA
Federal Bldg., Rm. 474
Midwest Archeological Ctr.
Lincoln, NE 68508

Activity: Application for Employment

Levels: Grades 3-8

Subjects: Language Arts, Social Studies, Science

Objectives: The students will (1) consider skills and knowledge needed to be an archeologist and (2) organize information.

PREPARATION:

Background: This activity will encourage the students to think about the traits and skills needed to be a professional archeologist. It will also encourage them to evaluate their own potential and how to market their skills.

Materials: Activity Sheet or questions on the board.

Procedures: (1) Have students complete a sample application to assist with an archeological investigation.
                 (2) Select a panel of three students to read the applications and, based on the applications, choose ten people to employ. Have the panel explain the criteria they used to make their selections.

Extension: Additional career information

                 "Sources of Information on Archeology"
                 Society for American Archeology
                 808 17th St. N.W. Suite 200
                 Washington, D.C. 20006

                 "Opportunities in Historical Archeology" (25¢)
                 Society for Historical Archeology
                 Box 231033
                 Pleasant Hill, CA 94523-1033

ACTIVITY SHEET

Name ____ Date ____________________________

APPLICATION TO ASSIST ON A
ARCHEOLOGICAL INVESTIGATION

NAME

LAST ______________ FIRST ____________ MIDDLE __________

ADDRESS ____

PHONE NUMBER ____

PERSONAL QUALIFICATIONS

____

____

____

EDUCATION

____

____

____

RELATED EXPERIENCE

____

____

____

LIST 3 REFERENCES

____

____

____

GLOSSARY

animism–a belief in which natural phenomena and animate and inanimate things are thought to possess a soul.

antebellum–before the Civil War (pre 1861).

archeology (archaeology)–the scientific study of past human life through human remains.

arrow–a straight, thin shaft shot from a bow with a pointed head at one end and feathers at the other.

artifacts–any object made or modified by a human.

assemblage–a collection of artifacts (often representing a cultural time period).

Atakapan–languages spoken by groups located in southwestern Louisiana.

Athapaskan–languages spoken by Navajos and Apaches.

atlatl–a spear thrower.

attribute–a well-defined feature of an artifact that cannot be divided.

awl–a sharp-pointed bone tool.

B.P.–before the present, which is dated at 1950.

band–a small hunting-gathering society with no status distinctions other than those based on age and sex.

biotic–referring to animal and plant life.

boatstone–a canoe-shaped ground stone artifact which may have been used as a atlatl weight.

bolas–stones attached to a rope used to catch animals by entangling the legs.

cache pit–a special storage place.

cairn–a mound of stones usually placed for directional or ceremonial purposes.

celts–a ground stone tool having one end shaped like a hatchet.

ceramics–articles made from clay and hardened by firing.

cert–a stone formed in limestone; widely used in making prehistoric tools.

chronological markers–artifacts with certain traits which are judged to represent a change in time periods.

chronology–the science that deals with determining the dates and order of events.

confluence–the point where two or more streams flow together.

context–the relationship of artifacts and other cultural remains to each other and to the surrounding soil deposits.

contiguous–touching or sharing an edge.

coordinate–one of an ordered set of numbers that give the location of a point.

cultivate–to grow and tend.

culture–a way of life for a group of people; learned behavior.

custom–repeated practice or convention used by a group of people.

dart–an arrow-like missile thrown by hand or atlatl.

date–to determine age, time, or origin of something.

deflector–a slab or stone placed so that drafts will be directed away from a hearth.

dendrochronology–tree-ring dating.

diagnostic–a distinctive mark or characteristic which permits assigning an artifact to a particular time or culture.

ecofact–an object from nature.

ecology–the science of the relationship between living things and their environment.

elevation–the depth or height from a fixed point.

empresorial –having the form of an agreement to recruit settlers and build a settlement.

ethnology–the study of the lifeways of a people or group by an observer who is sometimes a member of another culture.

ethnohistoric–descriptions of contemporary historic cultures.

excavation–systematic digging and recording.

exotic –unusual or rare for that culture; often acquired by trade.

fauna–animals.

feature–cultural remains which stay together and are more complex than a single artifact; examples are storage pits, fire hearths, burials, or cooking pits.

flaking–the way in which fracturing of stone produces needed tools and projectile points.

flora–plants.

flotation–a technique for recovering plant remains by using water to separate small remains (seeds, bones, etc.) from the heavier soil deposit.

function–normal or proper activity or use of something.

gastroliths–a small, stony mass formed in the stomach.

grid–a network of uniformly spaced lines that divide a site into units.

grog–crushed pottery used as a tempering material.

hafted–attached in a special way.

hearth–floor or base of a fireplace or aboriginal cooking area.

horticulture–gardening.

incised–engraved; cut into with a sharp tool.

intrusive–intruding without permission.

in situ–in the original place or location.

inventory–detailed list of materials.

knapper–one who makes chipped stone tools.

lechuguilla–a small version of the century plant.

level–uniform vertical measurements with the uppermost usually called level 1.

lithic–stone, or made from stone.

littoral–relating to a shore or coastal region.

magnetometry –study of intensity and direction of magnetic fields.

maguey–the century plant.

majolica –tin-glazed earthenware often richly decorated and colored.

mano –a hand-held ground-stone tool used to process foods.

megafauna–large, now-extinct Pleistocene animals, such as the mammoth.

Marksville–a culture of the Lower Mississippi Valley.

metate –stone slab upon which foods are ground or otherwise processed.

micaceous–containing mica.

midden–refuse or trash pile; a modern midden is a land-fill.

migrate–to move regularly to a different region, especially at a particular time of year.

Mogollon–a prehistoric culture occupying a region of what is today part of Arizona, New Mexico, Sonora, and Chihuahua.

mott–a small stand of trees on a prairie.

occupation–the act of using a place.

olla –a wide-mouthed ceramic jar.

Paleoindian–late Pleistocene peoples in the Americas.

physical remains–material left after disintegration, loss or removal of other material.

pictographs–painted art forms on rock.

playas–shallow, ephemeral, clay-bottomed basins which hold precipitation.

Pleistocene–a geological period characterized by glacial advances and retreats, ending about 11,500 years ago.

polychrome–decorated with more than one color.

prehistoric–before written records (in Texas before 1500).

presidio–a garrison established by the Spanish.

profile–a vertical view of a unit that shows the various exposed layers.

protohistoric–period of time just before recorded history.

provenience–exact location in three dimensions.

Puebloan–coming from one or more of the northern Rio Grande pueblos.

punctates–depressions in various shapes and made by various means.

radiocarbon dating–a frequently used method of dating based on measuring the decay of the radioactive isotope of carbon (C14) to stable nitrogen (N14).

rancheria –a settlement composed of individual dwellings of extended families.

red ocher–iron oxide mixed with sand and clay and used as a coloring pigment, often ceremonially.

retainer–a servant or attendant.

replicate–to reproduce or copy as accurately as possible.

room block–rooms with contiguous walls.

savanna–a flat grassland.

scapula–the large bone that forms the back part of the shoulder.

scraper–a chipped tool used in processing vegetal or animal materials.

screen–to separate with a sieve, usually means to separate soil from artifacts.

seasonal rounds–the trips made to obtain food resources in season.

sedentism–the condition of not being mobile or nomadic.

shaft straightner–a piece of stone or bone used to straighten dart or arrow shafts.

sherd–a fragment or piece of pottery.

site–any place that has the remains of past human activity.

sotol–a plant with long slender leaves edged with hooked thorns.

spear–a weapon consisting of a long shaft with a sharply pointed head.

stratified–in layers.

stratigraphy–the study of layers, or the layers in a site.

stratum–a layer.

subsistence–means of support, especially food-gathering.

survey–seeking and mapping artifacts on the surface in a systematic manner.

temper–material such as crushed bone or shell added to clay before pottery manufacture to reduce shrinkage and breakage during the drying and firing process.

tibia–the shin bone.

tool kit–a collection of materials used in manufacturing points, scrapers, etc., as well as a few of those implements in both finished and unfinished state.

topographic map–a plan which represents the exact physical features of a region.

travois –a sled-like carrying device pulled by a dog.

tumpline–a strap slung across the forehead or chest to support a load carried on the back.

typology–the process of classification of types or styles.

unit–a section of a site designated to be excavated and recorded (often 1m x 1m or 5 ft. x 5 ft.).

unslipped–without a clay and water solution applied to add color or make a smooth surface.

utilitarian–everyday or practical.

vegetal–pertaining to plants.

vessel–a hollow container, as a bowl, pitcher, or jar.

Waco sinker–a water worn pebble with notches on the ends, perhaps used as a sinker.

weir–a barrier placed in a stream to catch fish.

wickiup–a rounded, brush-covered shelter.

REFERENCES

Auel, Jean
1985 *The Mammoth Hunters*. Crown Publishers, New York.

Baylor, Byrd
1972 *When Clay Sings*. Macmillian Publishing Co., New York.

Caduto, Michael, and Joseph Bruchac
1988 *Keepers of the Earth*. Fulcrum, Inc., Golden, Colorado.

Campbell, Maria
1976 *People of the Buffalo*. Douglas and McIntyre, Vancouver, British Columbia.

Carter, Forrest
1976 *The Education of Little Tree*. University of New Mexico Press, Albuquerque, New Mexico.

Coffin, Tristram (editor)
1961 *Indian Tales of North America*. University of Texas Press, Austin, Texas.

Cork, Barbara, and Struan Reid
1984 *The Young Scientist Book of Archaeology*. Usborne Publishing Co., London, England.
Culin, Stewart
1975 *Games of the North American Indian*. Dover Publications, New York.

Fagan, Brian M.
1978 *In The Beginning: An Introduction to Archaeology*. Little, Brown, and Co., Boston, Massachusetts.

Field, Benjamin P., V
1989 U.S. History in a Box. *National Geographic*, 175 (5) 652-660.

Fox, Daniel E.
1983 *Traces of Texas History: Archeological Evidence of the Past 450 Years*. Corona Publishing Co., San Antonio, Texas.

Goble, Paul
1987 *Death of the Iron Horse*. Bradbury Press, New York.

Glubok, Shirley
1972 *The Art of the American Indian*. Harper & Row Publishing Co., New York.

Grosvenor, Gilbert M.
1974 *The World of the American Indian*. National Geographic Society, Washington, D.C.

Hackwell, John W.
1986 *Digging Into the Past*. Charles Scribner's Sons, New York.

Harrison, Michael
1984 *Archeology: Walney*. Fairfax County Park Authority, Fairfax County, Virginia.

Haviland, Virginia
1979 *North American Legends*. Wm. Collins Publisher, New York.

Hemion, Roger H.
1988 *Field and Laboratory Handbook*. Southern Texas Archaeological Association, San Antonio, Texas.

Hester, Thomas R.
1980 *Digging Into South Texas Prehistory: A Guide for Amateur Archaeologists*. Corona Publishing Co., San Antonio, Texas.

Hester, Thomas R., Robert F. Heizer, and John A. Graham
1975 *Field Methods in Archaeology*. Mayfield Publishing Co., Palo Alto, California.

Hole, Frank, and Robert F. Heizer
1965 *An Introduction to Prehistoric Archaeology*. Holt, Rinehart, and Winston, Inc., Dallas, Texas.

Kimball, Yeffe, and Jean Anderson
1965 *The Art of American Indian Cooking*. Doubleday, New York.

Kirkland, Forrest, and W. W. Newcomb, Jr.
1967 *The Rock Art of Texas Indians*. University of Texas Press, Austin, Texas.

La Farge, Oliver
1960 *The American Indian*. Golden Press, New York.

Lipetzky, Jerry
1982 *Dig 2: A Simulation in Archeology*. Interact, Lakeside, California.

Macaulay, David
1979 *Motel of Mysteries*. Houghton Mifflin Publishing Co., Boston, Massachusetts.

McHargue, Georgess, and Michael Roberts
1977 *A Field Guide to Conservation Archaeology in North America*. J.B. Lippincott Co., New York.

Minor, Marx
1972 *The American Indian Craft Book*. University of Nebraska Press, Lincoln, Nebraska.

Montgomery, David R.
    1985 *Indian Crafts and Skills*. Horizon Publishing, Bountiful, Utah.

Nathan, Robert
    1974 *The Weans*. Alfred A. Knopf Inc., New York.

National Geographic Society
    1985 *The Adventure of Archaeology*. National Geographic Society, Washington, DC.

Newcomb, W. W. Jr.
    1961 *The Indians of Texas: From Prehistoric to Modern Times*. University of Texas Press, Austin, Texas.

Nichols, Peter, and Belia Nicolas
    1988 *Archaeology: The Study of The Past*. Eakin Press, Austin, Texas.

Nichols, Peter, and Belia Nichols
    1990 *Mammoth Hunters to Mound Builders; Archaeology of North America*. Eakin Press, Austin, Texas.

Nunley, Parker
    1989 *A Field Guide to Archeological Sites of Texas*. Texas Monthly Press, Austin, Texas.

O'Dell, Scott
    1983 *Sing Down the Moon*. Houghton Mifflin Publishing Co., Boston, Massachusetts.

Pine, Tillie S.
    1957 *The Indians Knew*. Scholastic Inc., New York.

Rice, Prudence (editor)
    1984 *Pots and Potters: Current Approaches in Ceramic Archaeology*. Monograph 24, Institute of Archaeology, University of California at Los Angeles, Los Angeles, California.

Richter, Conrad
    1953 *The Light in the Forest*. Alfred A. Knopf Inc., New York.

Robson, Lucia St Clair
    1982 *Ride the Wind*. Ballantine Books, New York.

Saloman, Julian Harris
    1927 *The Book of Indian Crafts and Indian Lore*. Harper and Brothers, New York.

Shafer, Harry J.
    1983 *Ancient Texans: Rock Art and Lifeways Along the Lower Pecos*. Texas Monthly Press, Austin, Texas.

Spradley, James P. and Michael A. Rynkiewich
 1975 *The Nacirema: Readings on American Culture.* Little, Brown, and Co., Boston, Massachusetts.

Speare, Elizabeth George
 1983 *The Sign of the Beaver.* Houghton Mifflin Publishing Co., Boston, Massachusetts.

Turner, Ellen Sue, and Thomas R. Hester
 1985 *A Field Guide to Stone Artifacts of Texas Indians.* Texas Monthly Press, Austin, Texas.

Vander-Meulen, Susan
 1983 *The Indian Years.* Texas Historical Commission, Austin, Texas.

Warren, Betsy
 1971 *Indians Who Lived in Texas.* Steck - Vaughn, Austin, Texas.

Weitzman, David
 1975 *My Backyard History Book.* Little Brown and Co., Boston, Massachusetts.

Zappler, Georg and Helen Simons
 1984 *The Years of Exploration.* Texas Historical Commission, Austin, Texas.

JUVENILE FICTION

Cruvon, Margret
1973   *I Heard the Owl Call My Name*. Dell Publishing, New York.

The story of a young man's mission to a remote village of the Northwestern Indians. Mutual love and repect grow as they solve dilemmas together.

Doughty, Wayne Dyre
1966   *Crimson Moccasins*. Harper and Row, New York.

An adventure story of an Indian youth's trials in discovering who he is. The book is set in the mid-West in the late 1700s during the French and Indian War.

Hillerman, Tony
1972   *The Boy Who Made the Dragonfly*. Dell Publishing, New York.

A Zuni myth about a drought in the Southwest and a little boy who saves his people.

LaFarge, Oliver
1929   *Laughing Boy*. Houghton Mifflin Co., Boston, Massachusetts.

A dramatic tale of the native American's struggle to survive the intrusion of white man into Navajo country.

McDermot, Gerald
1974   *Arrow to the Sun*. Viking Press, New York.

The qualities of Pueblo art are used to tell the universal myth of hero-quest and Indian reverence for the sun.

McHargue, Georgess
1982   *The Turquoise Toad Mystery*. Delacorte Press, New York.

This adventure mystery features a junior high youth on a dig in Arizona. It is an excellent story for preservation.

McNickle, D'Arcy
1954   *Runner in the Sun*. University of New Mexico, Albuquerque, New Mexico.

The story of cliff dwellers at the time of drought. The story line is woven around the journey of a boy into manhood (literally and figuratively).

Miles, Miska
    1971   *Annie and the Old One*. Little, Brown and Co., Boston, Massachusetts.

This book tells about a close-knit Navajo family and the grandmother's acceptance of the life cycle. The grand-daughter attempts to stop time in order to prolong her grandmother's life.

O'Dell, Scott
    1983   *Sing Down the Moon*. Houghton Mifflin Publishing, Boston, Massachusetts.

The story of Navajos near Canyon de Chelly as the migration to a reservation is forced on them. A young girl is captured and escapes from slavers and returns to the old ways of life. Set in the 1860s and told from the Native American viewpoint.

Richter, Conrad
    1953   *Light in the Forest*. Bantam, New York.

A novel about a white boy captured by the Indians. He faces a great dilemma when he is returned to his family.

Speare, Elizabeth George
    1957   *Calico Captive*. Dell Publishing Co., New York.

An exciting and romantic story of a young girl's capture in New Hampshire during the French and Indian War.

Speare, Elizabeth George
    1983   *The Sign of the Beaver*. Dell Publishing Co. New York.

Set in the 1700s, this survival story relates the friendship that develops between a 13-year-old white boy and a resourceful Indian boy. The story provides good description of both frontier life and Indian culture.

MAGAZINES

Anthro Notes—Newsletter for Teachers
Dept. of Anthropology
Smithsonian Institute
Washington, D.C. 20560

Archaeology
Subscription Service
Box 50260
Boulder, Colorado 80321

Biblical Archaeology Review
Box 10757
Des Moines, Iowa 50347

Discovery
Box 359087
Palm Coast, Florida 32035

Expedition: The Magazine of Archaeology/Anthropology
University Museum—University of Pennsylvania
33rd and Spruce
Philadelphia, Pennsylvania 19104

National Geographic
Box 2895
Washington, D.C. 20077-9960

Natural History
American Museum of Natural History
Central Park West at 79
New York, New York 10024

Omni
Box 3026
Harlan, Iowa 5159

Scientific American
415 Madison Ave.
New York, New York 10017

Smithsonian Magazine
900 Jefferson Dr.
Washington, D.C. 20560

ARTICLES ON TEACHING ARCHEOLOGY

Carroll, Rivers Fowlkes
    1987   Schoolyard Archaeology. *The Social Studies* 78 (March/April) 67-75.
             Elementary school, 6th grade.

Catalina, Lynn J.
    1983   Digging into Hometown. *Cobblestone Magazine* 4 (June) 0-13.
             History magazine for children ages 8-14.

Cotter, John L.
    1979   Archaeologists of the Future: High Schools Discover Archaeology. *Archaeology* (Jan/Feb):29-35.
             High school program.

Dyer, James
    1983   *Teaching Archaeology in Schools.* Shire Publications, United Kingdom.
             British program for elementary and secondary schools.

Onderdonk, Richard
    1986   Piaget and Archaeology. *Archaeology* (Nov/Dec) 80.
             High school level teaching.

Passe, J. and Passe, M.
    1985   Archeology: A Unit to Promote Thinking Skills. *Social Studies* 76 (Nov/Dec) 238-239.
             Elementary level teaching.

Watts, Lou Ellen
    1985   They Dig Archaeology. *Science and Children* 23(Sept) 5-9.
             Elementary school, 6th grade.

TEACHING UNITS

Doherty, Edith, et al. *Stones and Bones: Archaeology* (1981) $22.95, Synergetics, Box 84, East Windsor Hill, Connecticut 06028.

Haas, Blakely, "Archeology: Man and His Culture" in *Ideas for Teaching Gifted Students Social Studies* (1982) Multi Media Arts, Box 180626, Austin, Texas 78718-0626.

Hawkins, Nancy, *Classroom Archaeology* (1984) Division of Archaeology, Box 44247, Baton Rouge, Louisiana 70804.

Kopec, Diane R., *Discovering Maine's Prehistory Through Archaeology: An Interdisciplinary Curriculum Unit for Grades 5-8* (1987). Main Historic Preservation Commission, 55 Capitol Street, State House Station 65, Augusta, Maine 04333.

Lipetzky, Jerry, *Dig 2: A Simulation in Archeology* (1982) and *Time Capsule: An Interaction Unit Preserving a Record of Today's Culture for the Next Generation's Discovery and Analysis* (1978) Interact, Box 997e, Lakeside, California 92040. (619) 448-1474.

Neuman, Roberta, et al. *Sleuthing Through History: An Introduction to Archaeology* (1983) J. Weston Walch, publisher, Portland, Maine 04104.

Simmons, Jody, et al. *Archaeology Is More Than a Dig* (1985) Camp Cooper, Tucson Unified School District, Box 40400, Tuscon, Arizona 85717-0400.

Smith, Dave, *Site Anasazi: A Simulation* and *Site Wolstenholme Towne, Virginia* (1989) GSP Inc., 7426 N. Bradley Place, Tucson, Arizona 85741.

Stark, Rebecca, *Archaeology* (1986) Educational Impressions, Opportunities for Learning, 20417 Nordhoff St., Chatsworth, California 91311.

Sylvester, Diane, et al. *Mythology*Archeology*Architecture* (1982) The Learning Works, Opportunities for Learning, 20417 Nordhoff St., Chatsworth, Califorma 91311.

EXHIBITS, ARTIFACTS, COMPUTER SIMULATION, AND TOOLS

EXHIBIT FOR LOAN

FROM: Institute for Texan Cultures
Box 1226
San Antonio Texas 78294
(512) 226-7651

Archeology in Texas
Six standing panels illustrating cultural time periods in Texas as found by archeologists. Photographs, drawings, and artifacts tell the story from Paleoindian to early settlers.

COMPUTER SIMULATION

FROM: Athena Digital
2351 College Station, Suite 567
Athens, Georgia 30605

Adventures in Fugawiland

TOOLS

Forestry Supplies
Box 8397
Jackson, Michigan 39204
(601) 354-3565

ARTIFACTS FOR INSTRUCTION

Biblical Archaeology Society
3000 Connecticut, NW Suite 300
Washington, D.C. 20008

Center for American Archeology
Kampsville Archeological Center
Kampsville, Illinois 62053

Hubbard
2855 Sherman Road
Northbrook, Illinois 60062

Nasco
901 Janesville Avenue
Ft. Atkinson, Wisconsin 53538

Opportunities for Learning
20417 Nordhoff St.
Chatsworth, California 91311

Palestine Institute Museum
Pacific School of Religion
1798 Scenic Avenue
Berkley, California 94709

AUDIO VISUALS

FROM: National Geographic
Educational Services
Washington, D.C. 20036
1-800-368-2728

The Science of Archaeology
Digging Up American's Past
Search for Fossil Man
Atocha: Quest for Treasure
Bushmen of the Kalahari
Kalahari Desert People
Dr. Leakey and the Dawn of Man
Leakey
Preserving Egypt's Past
Egypt's Pyramids: Houses of Eternity
In the Shadow of Vesuvius

FROM: Social Studies School Service
Box 802
Culver City, California 90232-0802
1-800-421-4246

Evidence of the Past
Detectives with Degrees
Concepts of Archeology
Diving for Roman Plunder
Lost Relics of the Sea
Calypso's Search for Atlantis

FROM: Odyssey Service
Public Broadcasting Association
1256 Soldier's Field Road
Boston, Massachusetts 02135

Seeking the First American
The Incas
Other People's Garbage
The Chaco Legacy
The Ancient Mariners
Myths and Moundbuilders
Maya Lords of the Jungle

FROM: Colonial Williamsburg, AV Section
Box C
Williamsburg, Virginia 23187

Doorway to the Past
Search for A Century
The Williamsburg File

FROM: Interpark
1540 E. MacArthur
Cortez, Colorado 81321
(303) 565-7453

Flintknapping with Bruce Bradley, PhD.

LOCAL ARCHEOLOGICAL SOCIETIES

Bee County College Archeological Society
Box 387, Mathis, TX 78368

Bell County Archeological Society
202 Twelve Oaks, Temple, TX 76504

Big Bend Archeological Society
P.O. Box 613, Alpine, TX 79830

Brazosport Archaeological Society
Brazosport Museum of Natural Science
400 College Dr., Lake Jackson, TX 77566

Central Texas Archeological Society
4229 Mitchell Road, Waco, TX 76701

Coastal Bend Archeological Society
934 Shepard, Corpus Christi, TX 76412-3530

Collin County Archeological Society
Heard Natural Science Museum, Box 22 Rt. 6
McKinney, TX 75069   (214)542-5566

Concho Valley Archeological Society
c/o Palmer
2833 West Harris, San Angelo, TX 76901

Dallas Archeological Society
P.O. Box 8077, Dallas, TX 75205-8077
(214) 368-8290

Dawson County Archeological Society
1507 N. 11th, Lamesa, TX 79331

El Paso Archaeological Society
P.O. Box 4345, El Paso, TX 79914

Gaines County Archeological Society
Box 232, Seagraves, TX 79359

Galveston Archeological Society
4814 Crockett Blvd., Galveston, TX 77551

Houston Archeological Society
P.O. Box 6751, Houston, TX 77265
(713) 523-3431

Iraan Archeological Society
P.O. Box 183, Iraan, TX 79744

Midland Archeological Society
P.O. Box 4224, Midland, TX 79704

Nacogdoches Archeological Society
1519 Pearl St., Nacogdoches, TX 75961

Northeast Panhandle Archeological Society
P.O. Box 173, Perryton, TX 79370

Panhandle Archeological Society
P.O. Box 814, Amarillo, TX 79105

Red River Archeological Society
2312 Speedway, Wichita Falls, TX 76308

Southern Texas Archaeological Association
123 E. Crestline Dr., San Antonio, TX 78201

South Plains Archeological Society
P.O. 655, Floydada, TX 79235

Tarrant County Archeological Society
1654 Kemble Court, Ft. Worth, TX 76103

Travis County Archeological Society
c/o TARL, Balcones Research Laboratory
10100 Burnet Rd., Austin, TX 78758

Webb County Archeological Society
1003 Hill Place, Laredo, TX 78041

━TEXAS HISTORIC PARKS & SITES TO VISIT━

State Historical Parks

Fort Griffin	Route 1, Albany, TX 76480
Fort Richardson	P.O. Box 4, Jacksboro, TX 76056
Goliad/General Ignacio Zaragoza	P.O. Box 727, Goliad , TX 77968
Governor Hogg Shrine	Route 3, Park Road 45, Quitman, TX 75783
Hueco Tanks	Rural Route 8, Box 1, El Paso, TX 79935
Jim Hogg	Route 5, Box 80, Rusk, TX 75785
Lyndon B. Johnson	Box 238, Stonewall, TX 78671
Misson Tejas	Route 2, Box 108, Grapeland, TX 75844
Sabine Pass Battleground	1.5 mi SE of Sabine Pass, TX
San Jacinto Battleground/	
Battleship Texas	3523 Highway 1836, La Porte, TX 77571
Seminole Canyon	P.O. Box 820, Comstock, TX 78837
Stephen F. Austin	P.O. Box 125 San Felipe, TX 77473
Texas State Railroad	P.O. Box 39, Rusk, TX 75785
Varner-Hogg Plantation	Box 696, West Columbia, TX 77486
Washington-on-the-Brazos	Box 305, Washington, TX 77880
Confederate Reunion Grounds	c/o Fort Parker, Route 3, Box 95, Mexia, TX 76667
Admiral Nimitz	P.O. Box 777, Fredericksburg, TX 78624

State Historic Sites

Acton	6 mi SE of Granbury, TX
Caddoan Mounds	Route 2, Box 85c, Alto, TX 75925
Eisenhower Birthplace	208 East Day, Denison,TX 75020
Fannin Battleground	Fannin, TX 77960
Fort Lancaster	P.O. Box 306, Sheffield, TX 79781
Fort Leaton	P.O. Box 1220, Presidio, TX 79845
Fort McKavett	P.O. Box 867, Fort McKavett, TX 76841
Landmark Inn	P.O. Box 577, Castroville, TX 78009
Ft. Lipantitlan	9 mi E of Orange Grove, TX
Magoffin Home	1120 Magoffin Avenue, El Paso, TX 79901
Monument Hill/Dreische Brewery	Route 1, Box 699, La Grange, TX 78945
Jose Antonio Navarro	229 South Laredo, San Antonio, TX 78207
Old Fort Parker	Route 3, Box 746, Groesbeck, TX 76642
Rancho de las Cabras Site*	5 mi S of Floresville, TX
San Jose Mission	Corner of Roosevelt Ave. and Mission Rd., San Antonio, TX
Fanthorp Inn	P.O. Box 296, Anderson, TX 77880
Starr Mansion	407 West Travis, Marshall, TX 75670
Lubbock Lake Landmark*	P.O. Box 2212, Lubbock, TX 79408

State Historic Structures

Fulton Mansion	P.O. Box 1859, Fulton, TX 78358
Port Isabel Lighthouse	P.O. Box 863, Port Isabel, TX 78578
Sam Bell Maxey House	821 South Church Street, Paris, TX 75460
Sabastopol House*	P.O. Box 1500, Seguin, TX 78156

* under development

SUMMARY OF
ANTIQUITIES CODE OF TEXAS

Cultural Resources

All antiquities which are discovered on public land are considered cultural resources. These resources may be shipwrecks, foundations of historic structures, stone tools used by Indians, or rock art. The Antiquities Code of Texas and the Texas Antiquities Committee were created by the legislature to ensure that cultural resources on public lands are not destroyed or exploited by a few and are protected for benefit of all the residents of Texas.

Construction Projects on Public Lands

Any project which involves ground disturbance on land of any state or local entity in Texas requires a review of the potential effect on archeological or historical resources. The staff of the Texas Antiquities Committee works with the developer or contractor to formulate a plan for appropriate mitigation, if cultural resources are identified during the evaluation process.

Permit Requirements

Permits to conduct archeological investigations of cultural resources are necessary on land within the public domain, that is, land which is owned and controlled by the local, state, or federal government. These permits are granted to qualified individuals and institutions who demonstrate the capability and willingness to obtain the maximum scientific, archeological, and educational information from such investigation. In addition, materials recovered from such investigations must be properly stored and available to the public for study.

Committee Responsibilities

The nine-member Antiquities Committee was created by legislation to be the legal custodian of all cultural resources, historic and prehistoric, within the public domain of the state of Texas. The TAC is mandated to maintain an inventory of materials recovered and retained by the state, identify and designate state archeological landmarks, disseminate information on TAC programs and policies, and protect and preserve the archeological and historical resources of Texas.

Legislation

The Antiquities Code of Texas was established by Senate Bill No. 58, Chapter 442, Government Code of Texas, and was redefined as the Texas Natural Resources Code of 1977, a formal revision of the statutes relating to the public domain, Title 9, Chapter 191 of the Resource Code pertains to the Antiquities Committee. Further revisions to the Antiquities Code were added in the Sunset Review process as reflected in Senate Bill 231 enacted by the legislature in 1983 and in House Bill 2056 in 1987.

For additional information concerning permits and copies of the General Rules of Practice and Procedure, contact the Texas Antiquities Committee, P.O. Box 12276, Austin, TX 78711, (512) 463-6098.

INFORMATION FOR SITE REPORTING

When cultural remains are encountered by accident or survey, the site should be reported. Permission of the land owner always must be obtained before any survey or investigation is begun.

Records for recording a site include

(1) Archeological site data form - may be obtained from and returned to
Texas Archeological Research Laboratory
Balcones Research Center
10,000 Burnet Road
Austin, TX 78758

(2) Location of the site recorded on a topographic map from the U.S. Geological Survey

(3) Photographs of the area.

After the above information is sent to the Texas Archeological Research Laboratory (TARL), a trinomial number will be assigned to the site and entered into the permanent records. The person recording the site will then be notified of the number.

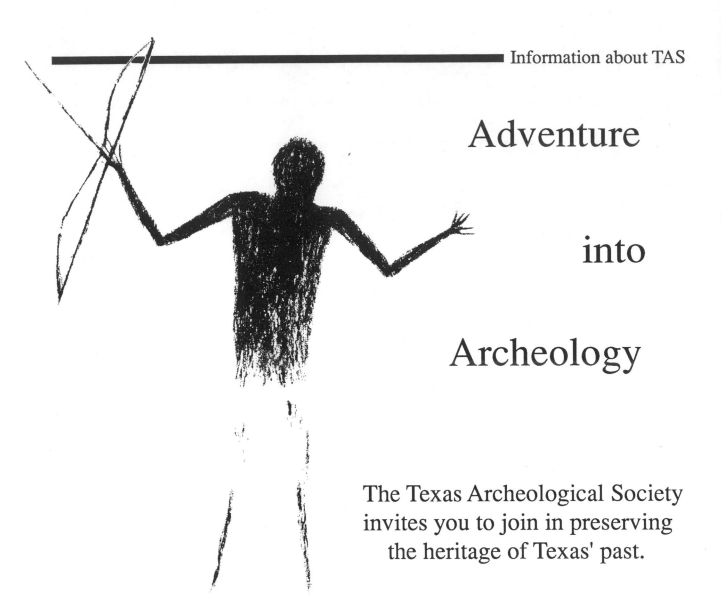

Adventure

into

Archeology

The Texas Archeological Society invites you to join in preserving the heritage of Texas' past.

The Texas Archeological Society was established in 1928 to encourage the study of archeology and to publish the results of archeological research in Texas and adjacent cultural areas.

Members of TAS receive the *Bulletin of the Texas Archeological Society*, a nationally recognized journal of regional archeology. In addition, the society's newsletter, *Texas Archeology*, is mailed to members four times each year. Newsletter articles highlight activities of interest to avocationals and professionals alike.

Membership in TAS entitles you to participate in annual meetings held in different cities of the state and in the annual summer field school. Both of these activities feature opportunities for learning archeological theory and methods.

For more information, contact: Texas Archeological Society
Center for Archaeological Research
The University of Texas at San Antonio
San Antonio, Texas 78285